10 SHORT STORIES

FOR THE ENGLISH LANGUAGE LEARNERS

Volume 3

Dušan Veselka

2018

This book contains 10 entertaining short stories that are suitable for both adolescent and adult readers.

The stories have a double plot structure and are enjoyable to read. All stories are written in simplified English and are stylistically written for those who wish to practise their English language by reading. The stories are simplified enough to be suitable for beginners and intermediate learners.

From the literary point of view, the writing style focuses on basic vocabulary and expressions that are used in the common speech. The sentences are short and with a clear context. Words and expressions that the reader might not be familiar with are highlighted, and their meanings are explained at the end of each story.

Contents

Family Reunion 10
Vocabulary 17
An Unwanted Painting 21
Vocabulary 29
A Friendship of Two Lonely Men 32
Vocabulary 47
A Cunning Bet 53
Vocabulary 63
A Business Trip 67
Vocabulary 73
A Bald Man's First Girlfriend 75
Vocabulary 86
Two Fishermen and Their Lonely Wives 90
Vocabulary 112
A Dating Advert Gone Wrong 119
Vocabulary 134
The Return of Bertha's Husband 138
Vocabulary 159
Twin Brothers and a Pretty Woman 166
Vocabulary 178

Family Reunion

Frank was an old man who lived in a small house. The house was **situated** in a **valley** with a river and a large forest. Frank spent very little time at home during the day. Every morning, he got up early, made **black coffee**, sat outside his house in the **patio** and thought about the day and what he **would** be doing.

Frank usually went **mushrooming** in the forest, or he went fishing in the river. Sometimes, when the weather was good, Frank worked on his house, did some necessary repairs, **chopped woods** for winter, worked on his garden or just went for a walk around the valley.

After spending all the days outside, Frank spent the evenings at home. First, after coming home, he cooked dinner and made some tea. Then, he sat in his sofa and read a book. It was in the evenings when Frank missed his family most.

Frank lived alone. His wife did not live anymore, and his children, who were already **grown-ups**, had moved away and had their own families. Frank had five children and they all lived in a city far away from the village where he lived.

Frank's children were visiting Frank very **rarely**, and Frank knew very little about his children's lives. He wished his children visited him more often, at least once a year on Christmas when he felt alone the most. Frank could not visit his children himself. He did not have a car because he had **poor eyesight**, and there were no bus or train services in his village.

Frank often wrote letters to his children. He was **curious** about how they were, he asked about their lives, their work and their children – Frank's grandchildren. Every time Frank wrote to his children, he asked them to come to visit him. But Frank received letters from his children very rarely.

From time to time, Frank went to the **local** pub. There, he ordered a pint of **ale** or **bitter** and talked to his friends. One night, when Frank went to the pub, he ordered a pint of ale and sat down to a table where he joined one of his best friends, Walter.

First, Frank and Walter talked about **ordinary**, everyday things, as usual, but later, Frank started to complain to Walter that his children were visiting him so rarely. **As** they talked about Frank's family, Walter got an idea. He did not say anything to Frank about his idea but smiled and said to him that his family would come to visit him soon.

But Frank did not believe it. He just waved his hand, finished his ale, said goodbye to Walter and went home. Frank knew that Walter was a good man, and he just said to Frank that his children would come to visit him because Walter wanted to make him feel better.

*

Walter was Frank's best friend, and he knew Frank's family. He also knew where all Frank's children lived because Frank had talked to Walter about his children a lot. The day after he and Frank had met in the pub where Frank complained about his children, Walter decided to visit Frank's children and **put his plan into action**.

Walter got up early and **packed** his **suit** into a **rucksack**. Then, he sat on his bike and **cycled** to the distant city where Frank's children lived. He cycled for **hours and hours**, and later in the afternoon, he finally arrived.

When Walter arrived in the city, he locked his bike and went to the public toilet where he **got changed** into the suit he had packed into his rucksack. He also combed his hair, washed his hands and put on perfume.

When Walter walked out of the public toiled, wearing his best suit, he looked very **smart**. Walter was ready to visit Frank's children and surprise them with the purpose of his visit.

After a few hours of walking around the city, Walter finally found one of Frank's children. It was a large house with two cars standing in front of it. Walter walked to the house and rang the bell. He did not wait long, and soon a man in his **forties** opened the door and asked Walter what he wanted.

Walter introduced himself as a lawyer and asked the man for a few minutes of his time because he needed to talk to him. The man, Frank's son, agreed and invited Walter into his house. Frank's son made some tea, and they sat down into a sofa and talked.

Walter said to Frank's son that he was Frank's **lawyer** and **worked on** Frank's **will**. Frank's son was shocked to hear that his father was writing a will and quickly asked if his father was fine. Walter assured him that Frank was fine, but he was already an old man and decided to write a will.

Later, Walter explained to Frank's son that because Frank had five children, he wanted to decide about which of his children would inherit his wealth. Frank wanted to give most of his money to his favourite son.

Frank's son was shock to hear about Frank's wealth. Frank's son thought that his father was poor, but Walter explained to him that although Frank lived **modestly throughout** his all life, he, in fact, had **managed** to save a lot of money.

Frank's son was really surprised about his father's wealth and said to Walter that he wanted to visit his father as soon as possible. Walter, still pretending that he was Frank's lawyer, said to Frank's son not to mention anything about the will in front of his father because it would look like he wanted to be nice to his father only because he wanted to be Frank's favourite child and get his wealth.

Frank's son quickly shook his head and said to Walter that he did not want to visit his father because of the will, but he wanted to visit him because he had not seen him for a long time. Frank's son also said to Walter that he **would** not mention the will. Walter smiled, **shook** Frank's son's **hand** and left.

Walter visited all Frank's children and told them the same thing he had said to the Frank's son who he had visited first. All Frank's children suddenly wanted to go to visit their father. They also promised to pretend that they did not know anything about the will.

Walter was happy. After he had visited all Frank's children, he went back to the public toilet, got changed into his old clothes, unlocked his bike and cycled back home.

When he arrived in his village later that day, Walter went to the local pub. There, he saw Frank, sitting alone at a large table. Frank looked very sad again, but when Walter came to him, he smiled, bought him a pint of ale and tried to **cheer him up**.

Whatever Walter tried to cheer Frank up, it was **of no use**. But Walter did not mind because he knew that soon Frank's children were going to visit him which was going to make Frank very happy.

*

Frank was still asleep, when suddenly loud **knocking** on the door of his house woke him up. When he opened his eyes, he listened if someone would knock on the door again. And so they did. When someone knocked on his door again, Frank jumped out of his bed, quickly put on some clothes and went to answer the door.

It was a shock for Frank to see one of his sons. His son smiled at him and walked inside. Frank was very happy and hugged his son. Then, he offered him some food, and they sat into a sofa and talked.

As they talked, suddenly someone knocked on Frank's door again. Frank and his soon looked each other, both **wondering** who it might have been. When Frank heard knocking on the door again, he jumped out of the sofa and quickly went to answer the door.

Frank opened the door and was shocked again to see who it was. It was his other son. Frank was happy to see him and invited him inside. He also offered him some food and drink, and they all sat together in a sofa.

That day, the rest of Frank's family arrived to visit him. Frank did not know what had happened and why all of his children came to visit him, but it was the first time Frank was with all of his children since they had all moved out. Frank was very happy.

Vocabulary

reunion – the act of coming together again

situated – to be positioned; to be located

valley – a low area of land between hills

black coffee – coffee without milk (Coffee with milk is called 'white coffee')

patio – a paved outdoor area connected to a house

would – the expression of the future time in the context of the past
– The word 'will' is used to express the future time: 'He will do it'. In the past context, you use 'would' instead of 'will': 'He said that he would do it.
The word 'would' is also used to express conditionality or possibility.

mushrooming – the act of picking mushrooms

chop – to cut

wood – the material from trees

grown-up – an adult, not a child

rarely – not often; sometimes

poor eyesight – a bad ability to see

curious – interested

local – relating to a certain location or neighbourhood

ale – a kind of beer (white and heavier than lager)

bitter – a kind of beer (more bitter and heavier than lager)

ordinary – usual; everyday

as – while; during the time when

put something into action – to make happen; to carry out what had been planned

pack – choose, select and collect clothes and put them into a suitcase (usually because of travelling somewhere)

suit – formal clothes

rucksack – a bag worn on a back

cycle – to ride a bicycle

hours and hours – a lot of hours (the conjunction 'and' multiplies the meaning of the words it connects)

get changed – to change the clothes someone wears
look smart – to look formal, neat and elegant

in someone's forties – When someone is in his forties, he is at the age between forty and fifty.

lawyer – a professional who practices law (legal rules)

work on – When someone works on something, he wants to achieve something.

will – a legal document declaring someone's wishes and plans of their properties after their death

modestly – without spending too much money

throughout – during the whole time

manage – to achieve a goal

shake hands – People shake their hands when they clasp each other's right hands to express agreement (or mutual respect).

cheer someone up – to make someone happier / less sad

of no use – useless; pointless; to no avail; fruitless; vain

and so something happened – and exactly that happened; something happened as expected or was suggested

wonder – to think; to speculate; to ponder; to muse; to contemplate

- You wonder about something when you are puzzled and think about something that might not make sense or want to solve.

An Unwanted Painting

Tim and Zoe, a newly **married** couple, bought a new house, and as soon as they bought a few pieces of **furniture**, they **moved in**. They only had a bed, sofa and a kitchen table with four chairs, but it was enough for them to enjoy living in their new house.

When Tim's parents visited them in their new house, they brought a present for them. Even though the present was **wrapped**, it was obvious to Tim and his wife Zoe what it was.

It was a large painting. Tim and Zoe were not very happy to see that Tim's parents wanted to give them a painting as a present but hoped that they would like it. They thanked them for the present and unwrapped it.

When Tim and Zoe looked at the painting, they did not say anything. They did not like the painting at all but did not want to say that to Tim's parents. Zoe was the first one to react and turned towards Tim's parents and thanked them for the nice present. Then, Tim pretended to be happy about the painting, smiled, lifted it up, looked at it closely and thanked his parents for the present.

Tim's parents were happy that Tim and Zoe liked the painting and hoped that they would hang it on the wall in their **living room**. Because they wanted to be polite and make Tim's parents happy, Tim and Zoe accepted the painting and agreed to hang it in their living room.

When Tim's parents left the house, Tim and Zoe were thinking about what to do. They did not like the painting and did not want it in their living room. The painting was **depicting** an old building, and both the painting and the frame were old. But Tim and Zoe wanted to buy modern furniture and make their new house look modern. Therefore, the old painting would not **fit** in their living room.

Tim and Zoe also could not understand why Tim's parents had decided to give them such an old and ugly painting. Tim's parents were rich and could afford to buy a nice and modern painting.

After some time, Tim and Zoe stopped talking and thinking about the painting, but because they did not want to disappoint Tim's parents and wanted to make them happy, they hanged the painting above their sofa in the living room.

But the longer they had the painting in their living room, the more they hated it. They tried to hang it on different walls where they would not see it so well, but wherever they hanged it, they could see it clearly. Also, although they did not like the painting, it **kept** attracting their eyes, and they looked at the painting every time as soon as they entered the living room.

With time, Tim and Zoe bought **more and more** furniture, and the more furniture they had, the less the painting fitted in their house. One day, when they were shopping for more furniture, they **came across** a shop where they were selling paintings. They saw a large and modern painting which they liked a lot, and after a few minutes of thinking and hesitating, they decided to buy it.

As soon as they came home with the new painting, they removed the old painting they had got from Tim's parents and replaced it with the new painting they had bought in the shop. Tim and Zoe absolutely loved the new painting and wanted to keep it on the wall in the living room.

One thing they needed to decide about was where they could put the old painting they had got from Tim's parents. Again, Tim and Zoe tried to hang the painting on different walls in the living room, but it did not fit anywhere. They tried to hang it in different rooms, but it did not fit there either.

In the end, Tim decided to tell his parents that although they loved the painting, it did not fit in their house, and they decided to replace it with a better fitting painting.

They knew that Tim's parents were going to be upset, but Zoe agreed with Tim that they should tell his parents.

Because they did not want to tell Tim's parents that they did not like the painting, they decided to tell them that the painting simply did not fit in their house. The painting was old, depicting an old historical building, while their house was new and modern, and even their furniture and the style of their **household** was modern.

Tim and Zoe invited Tim's parents for dinner one day so that they could tell them about the painting. Zoe cooked what she knew Tim's parents liked and also bought a bottle of wine. It was Sunday afternoon, and when Tim's parents arrived, Tim showed them their new painting and pointed out how well it fitted in their living room.

Tim's parents said that they liked the painting but noticed that Tim and Zoe bought the new painting to replace the old one. They were not happy to see that Tim and Zoe had bought a new painting but did not show it and looked like they did not mind. Tim's mother told Tim and Zoe that they should keep the old painting anyway, just in case they decided to hang it on a wall sometime in the future.

Tim and Zoe agreed to keep the painting and also agreed that maybe one day they would have a space for the painting somewhere. The rest of the evening was very

awkward, and as soon as they finished the dinner, Tim's parents left.

Tim and Zoe felt relieved that Tim's parents knew about their new painting, and they did not have to have the old painting on the wall anymore. But they could see that Tim's parents were unhappy that they did not keep the painting they had got from them on the wall in the living room.

Almost every day, Tim and Zoe talked about the old painting and wondered what to do with it. They did not have a space to store it properly and always had it hidden behind a piece of furniture.

One day, Tim and Zoe decided to sell the old painting even though it was a present and they had promised to Tim's parents that they would keep it. They did not want to keep it at home because they knew that they would never hang it on a wall in their house.

The next day, after they decided to sell it, Tim and Zoe wrapped the old painting and went to the local second-hand shop. There, a young and inexperienced man looked at the painting and checked it around to see if it was not damaged. After a few minutes looking at the painting, he offered them a price.

The price was very low, and Tim and Zoe were surprised that the man in the second-hand shop offered them so little. But because they did not like the painting and did not want to keep it, they accepted the price and sold it. When Tim and Zoe came home, they were happy that it **was all over** and that they had **got rid of** the painting at last.

Tim and Zoe did not know the city where they had bought their house very well yet, and they often walked the streets to get to know the city better.

One day, Tim and Zoe walked past a gallery. The gallery was an old, historical building with large windows. They could see a lot of paintings inside through the windows and decided to visit it.

They walked inside the gallery. It was very quiet inside, and there was no one there. The gallery had very large rooms with high ceilings, and there were paintings everywhere on the walls. Tim and Zoe walked around slowly and quietly, looking at all the paintings.

Most of the paintings had **price tags** underneath them with a short description of the paintings. When Tim and Zoe saw the prices, they were **shaking their heads**. Because they did not understand **fine arts**, they could not understand how all the paintings could be so expensive.

There were a few rooms in the gallery with one room **underground**. Tim and Zoe walked from one room to another, and, in the end, they visited the underground room. The underground room was dark, and there was only one painting hanging on the wall at the back of the room.

A **dim** light was shining on the painting from above. Tim and Zoe **stood still**, **staring** at the painting. It was a large painting and looked very **impressive** in the dark room with the dim light shining on it. Although Tim and Zoe did not understand fine arts, they knew that the painting in the dark room was a great **work of art**.

As Tim and Zoe looked at the painting, Tim quietly said that the painting looked like the old painting they had once got from his parents as a present. Zoe replied that it could not be the same painting, because they sold the painting in a cheap second-hand shop. It was impossible that their cheap painting would appear in such an expensive gallery.

Tim and Zoe moved closer to the painting to see if it really was their old painting. They could not believe it; it really was the old painting they had got from Tim's parents. They did not know what to say and just quietly kept looking at it.

As they were looking at the painting, Zoe read the description of the painting that was underneath it. The description read that the painting had been believed to be lost, but it was found in a local second-hand shop. Then, Zoe read the description of the painting. In the end, she read the price tag next to it.

Zoe could not believe what the price was, and she came closer to see the price better. As soon as she had a better look at it, she **shrieked** and **fainted**. Tim **got hold of** her quickly and laid her on the floor.

Tim did not understand what had happened. Zoe looked at the description and the price tag and suddenly fainted. Tim was curious what the description read and what the price was. He left Zoe on the floor, slowly got up, walked towards the painting and read the description. Then, he looked at the price tag. As soon as he saw the price, he fainted as well and fell on the floor.

Tim and Zoe were lying on the floor next to each other, in front of the old painting they had once had but decided to sell.

Vocabulary

married – a wife and a husband are a couple who are married; When a man and a woman get married, they become a husband and wife.

furniture – movable articles in rooms, usually made of wood that provide storage and comfort (for example a wardrobe, table, chair, and so on)

move in – When you buy a house and you move in, it means that you start living there.

wrapped – When you give a present to someone, you wrap it

living room – the main room in a house where people

depict – to give a description; to show (in a picture); to make a portrait

fit – to be suitable; to be appropriate

keep (doing something) – to continue (doing something)

with time – during time; after some time; in some time

more and more – continuously more (the conjunction 'and' multiplies the meaning of the words it connects)

household – the established of a house / home

awkward – not at ease socially

be all over – to be gone; to be finished

get rid of – When you own something and you get rid of it, you do not own it anymore.

price tag – a little label with a price on it

shake hands – People shake their hands when they clasp each other's right hands to express agreement (or mutual respect).

fine arts – creative arts to be appreciated for their imaginative, aesthetic or intellectual content such as painting

underground – beneath the surface or the ground

dim – not bright

stand still – to stand without moving

stare – to look with focus and with eyes wide open

impressive – of a strong effect or impression

work of art – something artistic that was created to be appreciated for its intellectual content such as painting

shriek – to cry; to shout; to yell

faint – to lose consciousness (and then usually fall on the ground); to pass out from weakness or emotional distress

get hold of – to grab; to hold; to get (something); to grasp

A Friendship of Two Lonely Men

It was late at night, but Mat could not sleep. There was a storm outside with loud **thunders** and bright **lightnings**. He was **tossing about** in bed, and after a while, he decided to get up.

He slowly got out of his bed, looked out of the window and watched the rain for a few minutes. It had been raining **constantly** for the last two weeks, and Mat had spent the whole two weeks in his house.

Mat lived alone. His wife did not live anymore, and he did not have any children. Quite often, Mat felt lonely in his house. He was old and did not go out so often, and he spent most of the time in his house or in his garden.

Sometimes, Mat wished that he had someone to talk to. His neighbours were young people who spent their time at work and with their children, and he did not meet them often. Sometimes, Mat went to the local pub where he met his friends, but the pub was far away, and Mat did not want to walk there too often.

Looking out of the window, Mat quietly complained about the rain and left the bedroom. He went to the bathroom and washed his face. Then, he made a cup of coffee and walked to the **living room** where he sat into an armchair and switched on the TV.

All TV channels were **reporting** on the storm and heavy rain, as well as **floods** that were **occurring** in the neighbouring villages. Mat's house, as well as the whole village where Mat lived, was on top of a hill and did not get flooded.

As he watched all the news and reports on the floods in the neighbouring villages, he felt sorry for the people who had lost their houses or had their houses damaged and did not have anywhere to live. He would like to help these people but did not know how to.

In some villages, the floods were already **subsiding**, but in others, the floods were still rising. Some people needed help with cleaning and refurbishing, some needed help with moving their furniture, but Mat was too old to help the people with hard physical work.

He switched the TV off and started reading a newspaper he had on a small **coffee table** next to the armchair where he was sitting. Same as all the TV channels, the newspaper was also reporting on the floods and people losing their homes.

Mat felt very sad and put the newspaper down. He got up, walked around the house slowly and thought about how he could help the people affected by the floods. He walked through the large corridor, went to all his rooms, when he suddenly got an idea.

He **stood still** for a while, thought about the idea, and after a few seconds, he quickly went to the living room. There, he **grabbed** the newspaper he had read before and was quickly **leafing through**.

Mat remembered to see an **advert** in the newspaper with an address where people who would like to help those affected by the floods could send a letter and offer their help.

Mat found the advert and went to the kitchen where he put the newspaper on a **dinner table**. Then, he took a sheet of paper and a pen, sat down to the table and started to write.

Mat had a large house with a spare bedroom. He decided to offer the spare bedroom to a person who did not have a home and needed to live somewhere **temporarily**. He explained in the letter that he was an **elderly** man and lived alone, and he also **described** the house where he lived, as well as the room he was offering.

Mat wrote the letter, folded the paper, put it into an envelope and wrote on it the address he had found in the newspaper. He smiled and felt good about the idea. Now, he thought, he could help someone.

It was early in the morning, but the post office was already open. Mat put on **wellington boots**, a jacket with a **hood**, grabbed an **umbrella** and left the house.

It was still raining outside, and Mat could also hear thunders in the distance. The post office was not too far away from his house, and Mat did not have to walk for long in the rain. It was still dark, and there was no one in the streets.

When Mat arrived at the post office, there was no one there either. He walked to the **counter** where he met his friend who worked there as a postman. The village where Mat lived was small and Mat knew everyone who lived there.

The postman was surprised to see Mat in the post office, especially so early in the morning, and he asked him what had brought him there. Mat showed the postman the letter which he had pulled out of his pocket and said to him that he wanted to **post** it.

The postman was surprised again to see that Mat wanted to post a letter. He knew that Mat did not have a family, and he did not have friends who lived far away and who he would be sending letters to. He asked Mat where he was posting the letter, and Mat explained to him that he wanted to help someone who did not have anywhere to live by offering his spare room to them.

The postman was shocked to hear that and said to Mat that it was a dangerous idea to take a stranger to his house. Mat disagreed. He **shook his head** and said that those who did not have anywhere to live and needed help were not dangerous.

Mat put the letter on the counter and asked the postman to send it to the address written on the envelope. The postman **shrugged his shoulders**, took the letter slowly and agreed to **deliver** it. Then, the postman said to Mat one more time to be careful. Mat replied to the postman not to worry and left the post office.

Mat was very **excited** and hoped that soon he **would** receive a reply from someone who would accept his help and come to live with him for some time. As soon as he came home from the post office, he went to the spare room in his house and started cleaning it and preparing it for someone to live there.

Days passed and Mat had not received any reply to his help offer yet. The weather was still bad, it was still raining and the floods in some areas were still rising. **More and more** people were losing their homes and did not have anywhere to live.

Mat was sitting in an armchair, reading a book, when suddenly the doorbell rang. Mat raised his head and looked towards the door. For a few seconds, Mat was wondering who it might have been. He never had visitors. When the doorbell rang for the second time, he thought that it might have been the postman. He got out of the armchair and quickly went to answer the door.

It was the postman as Mat had thought. His clothes were wet and when Mat opened the door, the postman took off his hat to **greet** him. Mat greeted the postman and invited him inside. The postman refused and said that he did not have time because had more letters to deliver to other people.

The postman pulled a letter out of his large bag and gave it to Mat. Mat took the letter, thanked the postman and closed the door. Mat was very happy that he received the letter because he believed that it must have been from someone to whom he offered his spare room. He quickly ran to the kitchen, opened the envelope and unfolded the letter.

Mat walked slowly around his house while he was reading the letter. As Mat had expected, the letter was from a man who replied to Mat's advert when he had offered his spare room to someone who needed somewhere to live.

The letter was from a man whose name was Ben. He was an elderly man who did not have anywhere to live. He was alone, a widower, and **had fallen out** with his children.

Mat smiled and quickly replied to Ben's letter. Ben soon replied back, and they agreed to meet in the local pub in Mat's village. The day of their meeting, Mat wanted to put on nice clothes, but because it was still raining outside, he put on wellington boots and a long coat to keep him dry. He took an umbrella and went to the pub.

Mat arrived in the pub a little earlier than when they had agreed. He bought a pint of **ale** and sat to a small table next to a window at the back of the pub. As soon as he sat down, a slim man with grey hair came to him and asked him if he was Mat.

Mat stood up, **nodded** and replied that, indeed, his name was Mat. The man with grey hair replied that his name was Ben. They **shook their hands**, Ben sat to the table next to Mat, ordered a pint of ale, and they started talking.

Mat and Ben talked and laughed and drank a few pints of ale. They talked about the past, their hobbies and everything interesting that had ever happened to them in their lives. Although Mat and Ben knew each other for only a couple of hours, they felt like they had known each other for years.

They finished their ales and went to Mat's house. Inside the house, Mat showed Ben the spare room where Ben would live. The room was **spacious**, clean and with nice furniture. There was everything Ben needed in the room. A large bed, a wardrobe, a chest of drawers, a small desk and an armchair.

Ben only had a suitcase with him, which contained a few pieces of clothes and one pair of shoes. That was everything Ben had owned. Mat felt sorry for Ben and tried to **cheer him up** by saying that **with time** he would be able to buy more clothes.

Mat suddenly realised that he had not eaten for several hours and offered Ben some food. Ben agreed and they both went to the kitchen. There, Mat opened a fridge and looked for some food. There was not much food in the fridge, except for a few sausages, a piece of butter, milk and a bit of cheese.

Mat felt **embarrassed** that he did not have any proper food at home and blamed himself that he had not thought about buying some, especially that day when Ben came to live with him. Mat took the sausages out of the fridge, cut two slices of bread and asked Ben if he would be happy with sausages and bread for dinner.

Ben saw the ingredients Mat had in his kitchen and asked Mat if he would like to have mashed potato with the sausages and a little bit of **gravy**. Mat looked at Ben, **shrugged his shoulders**, smiled and nodded. Ben took potatoes he had seen in the kitchen, cooked them and made **mash**. In the meantime, he **fried** the sausages and made gravy.

Mat liked Ben more and more. The more they talked and the more and the longer Mat knew Ben, the more he liked him. Mat enjoyed living with Ben, and he did not feel lonely anymore.

Mat and Ben spent all their time together, and they also did things together. They cooked, played cards and chess, worked in the garden, and they also worked on the house when some repairs were needed. There was a train station at the end of the village with a train service once a week, and sometimes Mat and Ben also travelled together. Mat and Ben soon became good friends.

The rain stopped a long time ago, and all floods in the neighbouring villages **subsided**. People affected by the floods were already working on repairing their houses so they could move in as soon as possible. But Ben never talked about his house and never talked about moving back in.

One evening, when Mat and Ben watched a TV report on people moving back to their houses after the flood water had subsided, Mat asked Ben if he would like to go and see his house. Also, Mat offered Ben his help with cleaning the house.

Ben replied to Mat that he would go and clean his house, but he wanted to do it himself, without Mat's help. Mat was surprised that Ben did not want Mat to go with him to see his house and help him with cleaning and refurbishing it.

Ben was explaining to Mat that he did not want him to do hard work. Ben also said to Mat that he had helped him a lot already by providing him with the room in his house and did not want to ask him for more help.

It seemed to Mat that Ben simply did not want to go and see his house. Mat also thought that Ben did not want to see his house damaged and needed more time to get ready to return back home.

Time passed, but Ben had not gone to see his house. From time to time, Mat asked Ben about his house, but Ben never wanted to talk about it. One day, when Ben **offered himself** to do the shopping and left the house, Mat went to Ben's room and found his **ID**. There was an address on the ID and Mat decided to go and see Ben's house himself.

When Ben came back home after doing the shopping, Mat **came up with an excuse** that the next day he needed to see his doctor who lived in the neighbouring village. Ben agreed and offered himself to prepare some food for Mat and himself so that they could have dinner together.

The next day, Mat got up early in the morning and went to see the local farmer. He asked the farmer if he could **give him a lift** to the neighbouring village. The farmer agreed and drove Mat to the village where he wanted to get.

There was a river in the village where Mat went to see Ben's house, and all the houses alongside the river were damaged by the flood water. Mat and the farmer were looking for Ben's house but could not find it. The farmer stopped the car, and Mat went to ask some people who worked on their house if they knew the address Mat was looking for.

The people **directed** Mat and the farmer to the address. It was on a hill where no houses had been affected by flood. Mat was surprised to see that Ben's house was among those that had not been flooded. As Mat and the farmer drove through the street of houses on the hill, they eventually found Ben's house.

The farmer stopped the car and waited inside. Mat got out of the car and walked to the house. **As** Mat approached the house, he heard people inside talking. He **knocked** on the door, and a young man opened the door.

Mat was surprised to see that someone lived in the house. Mat explained to the young man that he had thought that it was Ben's house and was surprised to see him there. The young man explained to Mat that he and his wife did not **own** the house, but they were renting it temporarily because their house had been damaged by the flood.

Mat was shocked to hear that and became very angry. He quickly ran to the car and asked the farmer to drive him back to his village. Mat did not speak with the farmer the whole way home, and when the farmer saw how angry Mat was, he did not ask him anything.

When they arrived in their village, Mat thanked the farmer for giving him a lift and quickly walked home. Mat opened the door and **slammed** it. Ben was in the kitchen, preparing food for himself and Mat. Ben said hello to Mat and asked him about his health and his visit at the doctor's.

Mat did not answer, but instead, he told Ben that he needed to talk to him. Ben could see that Mat was angry and was afraid to hear what had happened. Mat told Ben that he had gone to see his house and there was nothing wrong with it. Also, Mat told Ben that instead of him living in his own house, he had **tenants** there. Ben was renting his house to those who had been affected by floods, while Ben wanted to live with Mat as someone who did not have anywhere to live.

Before Ben managed to say anything and explain to Mat what had happened to his house, Mat asked him to leave. Ben was angry that Mat was shouting at him and asked him to leave without hearing any explanation. Ben packed his clothes into his case and left the house.

Mat could not believe that Ben had lied to him about not having anywhere to live. Ben, on the other hand, could not believe that Mat would not let him explain it to him.

Time passed, but Mat had not heard from Ben. Mat felt lonely again in his empty house, and he missed Ben a lot. After some time, Mat wanted to find Ben, apologise to him and talk to him again. Mat did not care anymore why Ben did not live in his house, and Mat wanted Ben to live with him again. Mat had enjoyed living with Ben and missed him as a friend.

Everything went back to normal for Mat. He got up late in the morning, made some coffee, read newspapers and later either watched TV or read a book. He thought about Ben every day.

One morning, someone rang the doorbell, and Mat went to answer the door. It was the postman who had a letter for him. Mat was curious about who had written him a letter. He went to the kitchen, took a knife and opened the envelope. There were two letters in the envelope. One was from a lawyer, and the other one was from Ben. Mat sat down into an armchair and slowly read the letters.

The letter from the lawyer read that Ben died, but before he died, he made had his **will** and left everything to Mat. In the second letter, which was from Ben, Ben explained that he had owned his house and had lived there with his son. When his son had moved out into his own house, Ben had rented out some rooms in the house to have some **income** while he still had lived in one room of the house as well. Ben had not **got on well** with the people, but because he could not have **terminated** the **tenants'** contract, he had decided to move out. For a while, Ben had lived in hotels and **bed and breakfasts**, but was quickly running out of money.

One day, Ben kept explaining, he saw an advert in the local newspaper where someone was offering his spare room to someone who needed somewhere to live. The advert did not **specify** that the person who needed somewhere to live had to be someone who had lost their house because of the flooding. Therefore, Ben had decided to reply.

Mat felt terrible. He offered Ben his spare room, Ben became his best friend, and then, he asked him to leave his house although he did not have anywhere else to live. And now, Ben was dead.

Mat started to cry but **carried on** reading the letter from Ben. Ben knew that Mat did not have much money and could not even afford proper food because his **pension** was too low. For that reason, Ben decided to leave his house to Mat. He could rent the house or sell it and make money for himself.

The last thing Ben wrote to Mat in his letter was where he was **buried** and that he would like Mat to come and visit his **grave** from time to time.

Vocabulary

lonely – sad because one has no friends or company

thunder – a loud noise coming from stormy clouds, preceded by a lightning

lightning – a very bright light caused by a friction of stormy clouds, followed by a thunder

toss about – to move frequently from side to side when in bed, usually during sleeping

constantly – all the time; non-stop; without interruption

living room – the main room in a house where people

report – to give information; a short account of the news; the act of informing

flood – When the level of water in a river gets too high (usually after a heavy rain) and covers dry areas where the water does a damage, it means that the dry areas are flooded.

occur – to come to pass; to be found to exist

as – while; during the time when
subside

coffee table – a low table, usually in a living room or dining room where coffee (or other drinks) are served

stand still – to stand without moving

grab – to take or grasp quickly or suddenly
leaf through

advert – a public promotion of a product or service

dinner table – a table where dinner (meals) is served and eaten

elderly – old; an old person or people

describe – to give a detailed account in words

wellington boot – high (knee-length), rubber, water-proof boots

hood – a covering for the head and neck with an opening for the face, usually part of a jacket or sweatshirt

umbrella – a foldable thing you hold in your hand that reaches above your head and covers your body when it rains

counter – a bar / low wall, usually in shops dividing the sellers and the shoppers.

- In a post office, the postman is behind a counter, and the customer is before the counter. The counter is between them.

post – to send a letter or parcel using the post office

shake someone's head – When you shake your head, you express disagreement by moving your head from left to right.

shrug someone's shoulders – When you shrug your shoulders, you lift them up to express certain thoughts or feelings according to the context (for example indifference, disinterest, unconcern, the lack of knowledge, and so on).

deliver – to bring to a destination

excited – emotional; aroused; affected by emotions

would – the expression of the future time in the context of the past
– The word 'will' is used to express the future time: 'He will do it'. In the past context, you use 'would' instead of 'will': 'He said that he would do it.
The word 'would' is also used to express conditionality or possibility.

more and more – continuously more (the conjunction 'and' multiplies the meaning of the words it connects)

greet – to say hello or goodbye

fall out (with someone) – to have a breach in a relation - When two friends fall out with each other, they are not friends anymore.

ale – a kind of beer (white and heavier than lager)

nod – to lower and raise the head to express agreement

shake hands – People shake their hands when they clasp each other's right hands to express agreement (or mutual respect).

spacious – having ample / large space

cheer up – to make happier (usually when someone sad)

with time – during time; after some time; in some time

embarrassed – to feel uneasy

gravy – a sauce made by mixing fat and juices from meat during cooking

mash – crushed cooked potatoes with butter and milk

fry – to cook in oil or on a pan

offer himself – When someone offers himself to do something, he asks the other person that he would like to do it.

ID – This abbreviation stands for 'identity card'. An identity card is a little card with personal information, which purpose is to identify the person who owns the card.

come up with an excuse – to make an excuse

give someone a lift – to pick someone up and drive them somewhere; to drive someone somewhere
- We want to go somewhere by car. We agree to meet in front of your house. I drive to your house where you wait for me, you get into my car, and we drive away. – In this case, I gave you a lift.

direct - to show a direction; to show the way

knock – to tap or hit loudly enough to be heard when someone wants to attract attention
– You knock on a door when you want someone to open the door.

own – to possess; to have (as a property)

temporarily – not permanently; for a limited period of time

slam – to close quickly, with force and loudly

tenant – a person who lives in a rented property (in a property he does not own but pays a rent to be allowed to live there)

will – a legal document declaring someone's wishes and plans of their properties after their death

income – a financial gain

get on well – When two people get on well together, they have a good relationship

terminate – to end, to bring to an end

bed and breakfast – a boarding house (similar to a hotel) where you can sleep and have breakfast

specify – to define clearly

carry on – to continue

pension – a regular payment

bury – to place in the ground
- When someone dies, they are buried by being placed deep in the ground.

grave – a place where a person is buried

A Cunning Bet

Eddie came home from work and went **straight** to the kitchen. There, he opened the fridge and pulled out a tray full of **sausages**, a plate of sliced **ham** and a plate of sliced smoked **bacon**. He also put a little bit of mustard on a small plate, cut a few slices of bread, and after he had fried the sausages and bacon, he started eating.

Eddie was very hungry and enjoyed the food. He ate fast and was **smacking his lips**. Eddie's wife, Sarah, heard him eating and came to meet him in the kitchen. When she saw Eddie eating so much food again, she sat down to the table next to him and, without saying anything for a while, she watched him eating.

Eddie looked at his wife, stopped eating for a moment and asked her why she was looking at him. Sarah started to complain to Eddie about how much he was eating again and how much weight he had gained recently. Sarah asked Eddie to **go on a diet** and start to **exercise** in order to **slim down**.

Eddie **sighed**, shook his head to **indicate** his wife that he was dismissing her complaining, and continued eating. As soon as he shook his head and started eating again, Sarah got very angry, left the table and walked towards the kitchen door. At the kitchen door, Sarah stopped, turned towards Eddie and said to him that there is a lot of work to do in the garden which she could not do herself because of her **backache**.

When Sarah left the kitchen, Eddie felt guilty and stopped eating. He thought about what Sarah had said to him about his weight and about the work that needed to be done in the garden. Eddie did not know what he would **hate** to do more, whether to reduce the amount of food and slim down or to do some work in the garden.

Eddie got up, walked to the kitchen window, looked out and thought about it for a while. First, he thought about **reducing** the amount of food and doing some exercise. Then, he thought about the work in the garden. Working in the garden meant **mowing** the grass, **sprucing** the trees, cutting **bushes**, **chopping** wood for winter, clearing away leaves and doing a lot of other work.

Eddie did not like either of those two ideas. He did not want to eat less and slim down, and he did not want to work in the garden. At that moment, Eddie did not want to eat anymore because his wife had made him feel bad. For that reason, Eddie put the food back in the fridge and went to the **local** pub.

In the pub, Eddie bought a **pint** of beer and joined one of his friends who was sitting at a table not far from the bar. Eddie's friend noticed how sad Eddie looked and asked him what had happened. Eddie told him about the conversation he had had with his wife about him slimming down and doing a lot of work in the garden.

Eddie liked food a lot and did not want to eat less and slim down. But he was also very lazy and did not want to work in the garden. He did not know what to do. Eddie's friend laughed at Eddie for a while, but then, he said to Eddie that he had similar problems at home. His wife also wanted him to eat less and do more work at home.

After some time, Eddie's friend stopped laughing at him and became more serious. They drank more beer and talked about Eddie's problems he had at home. After they drank a few beers, Eddie's friends asked Eddie what his wife would want more, him to slim down or to do the work in the garden. Eddie replied that his wife would prefer if Eddie slimmed down because she could ask their son to help her with the work in the garden. At that moment, Eddie's friend said to Eddie that he got an idea.

Eddie was interested in what idea his friend had got and wanted to hear that. He **drank up** his beer, hit the table with the empty pint, ordered another beer, sat closer to his friend and asked him what idea he had got.

Eddie's friend leaned towards Eddie and started explaining to him his idea. Eddie's friend started telling Eddie that his wife wanted him to slim down and to do some work in the garden. Eddie **nodded**. Then, Eddie's friend told Eddie that he should have made a bet with his wife.

To make a bet? Eddie asked. What bet? Eddie's friend told Eddie that he did not want to slim down, and he did not want to work in the garden either. Eddie nodded. Then, Eddie's friend said to Eddie that he should offer his wife a bet as a compromise: that he would slim down if she stopped asking him to do the work in the garden.

Eddie was not sure if he liked the idea. He did not want to slim down because he would have to eat less and do some exercise. Eddie said to his friend that it was not a great idea and that he would not make a bet with his wife about him slimming down.

But Eddie's friend smiled and said to Eddie that he knew a trick how he could win the bet without reducing his food and without exercising. Eddie was **curious** and listened again.

Eddie's friend explained the trick to Eddie. Before making the bet with his wife, Eddie had to eat a lot of food – much, much more than normal. Then, after the bet and shortly before **weighing** himself, he had to drink as much water as possible. Eddie smiled, and his friend continued explaining. One litre of water weighs about one kilogram. If Eddie drank for example three or four litres of water before weighing himself and without going to the toilet, he would immediately gain three or four kilograms. If he also ate a lot that day, he would gain even more. Then, at least one day before weighing himself again, Eddie would not eat or drink the whole day in order to lose as much weight as possible to make sure he would be about five kilograms lighter than before the first weighing.

Then, Eddie's friend said to Eddie that he should make a bet with his wife that he would lose five kilograms in a week. And if he succeeded, he would not have to work in the garden. Losing five kilograms of weight in a week would be a great **achievement**, and surely, his wife would accept the bet because she would be happy to see such an achievement from Eddie.

Eddie liked the idea of gaining weight before the first weighing, although he did not like the idea that he would have to stop eating before the second weighing. But Eddie's friend told him that if he **managed** not to eat one day, he would not have to do the work in the garden and his wife would be proud of him. Also, Sarah had never believed that Eddie could slim down so this could be a chance for Eddie to show to his wife that he could slim down if he wanted to.

Eddie quickly ordered two pints of beer, one for himself and one for his friend. Then, he smiled and said that he was going to make a bet with his wife.

Eddie finished his beer and went home. His wife was already asleep. He opened the fridge, took out a few schnitzels, cut a few slices of bread, sat down to the table and started eating. He thought about the bet and knew that he could win.

The next day in the morning, Eddie got up and went straight to the kitchen. He opened the fridge, took out a few sausages, a plate full of bacon, a handful of eggs, a cup of **mushrooms** and cooked himself large breakfast.

As every morning, Sarah came to the kitchen and as soon as she saw Eddie eating a lot of food, she complained about it. Eddie smiled and waited until Sarah started complaining about his weight. He did not have to wait too long. When Sarah saw how much Eddie was eating that morning, she quickly started complaining about it and said that he was eating more and more. And, as always, Sarah complained about Eddie's weight.

Eddie stopped eating and pretended that he was angry. He looked at Sarah and said to her that he could slim down any time he could. Sarah was surprised to hear that Eddie had said that, and for a few moments, she did not say anything. Then, she suddenly started laughing at Eddie and said that he could not slim down because he would never be able to eat less food.

At that time, when Eddie knew that it was the right moment, he offered Sarah to make a bet. Sarah stood still and look at Eddie without saying anything. Then, Eddie said that he could slim down five kilograms in one week. Sarah started laughing again and argued that it was impossible. Then, Eddie stood up, **held out his hand** and asked her to bet with him on that. Then, Eddie said to Sarah that if he managed to slim down five kilograms in one week, he would not have to do the work in the garden that she had asked him to do.

Sarah liked the idea of making a bet with Eddie, especially when it was about him slimming down. She wanted to see him on a diet and agreed. She did not believe that Eddie could slim down five kilograms in one week and was looking forward seeing Eddie working in their garden. Eddie and Sarah agreed on the bet, and they **shook their hands**.

Immediately, Sarah wanted to start counting the week since Eddie should start slimming down and brought **bath scales**. But Eddie did not want to weigh himself at that moment. First, he wanted to eat more, and then, he wanted to drink as much water as possible. He replied to Sarah that he wanted to finish his breakfast first. Sarah agreed, smiled and left the kitchen.

As Sarah was leaving the kitchen, she was saying to Eddie that he should stop eating the breakfast and start concentrating on slimming down instead. Then, Sarah said to Eddie to let her know when he was ready. Sarah was very excited about the bet.

After Sarah left the kitchen, Eddie went back to eating his breakfast. It was a lot of food, but he managed to eat it all. Then, he ate even more food, and when he could not eat any more, he started drinking a lot of water. When he could not hold any more food and water in his stomach, he shouted at Sarah to come to the kitchen and **witness** the weighing.

Eddie stood on the scales and weighed one hundred and twenty kilogrammes. He smiled because it was almost four kilogrammes more than his usual weight. He was confident that he would win the bet. He shouted at Sarah again and Sarah **shouted back** at Eddie that she was coming.

Eddie **waited and waited**, but Sarah was not coming. Sarah was in the garden looking around and writing down a list of what needed to be done. Eddie was feeling sick after the amount of food he had eaten and the amount of water he had drunk and shouted at Sarah again.

Sarah was in the middle of the list she was writing and asked Eddie to wait for a few minutes. Eddie was shocked. He could not wait because he was getting **more and more** sick. Eddie called Sarah one more time, but after a few seconds, before Sarah came, Eddie ran to the bathroom and **threw up**.

Sarah finished the list and came to the kitchen. But Eddie was not there. Sarah walked around the house but could not find him. She called Eddie and shouted where he was. Eddie did not reply. Sarah called Eddie again, but again, Eddie did not reply. Sarah wondered where Eddie could be and checked every room.

In the end, Sarah went to the bathroom where she found him. Eddie was sitting on the bath with his face wet. Sarah asked him what had happened and he replied that he got sick and threw up. Then, he washed his face and waited in the bathroom just in case he got sick again.

Sarah patted Eddie on the back and said to him that he had got sick because of the large amount of food he had eaten for breakfast. Eddie was very sad because he knew that after he had thrown up, he would not weigh so much anymore. Eddie shook his head and did not say anything. Sarah turned around and went to the kitchen. From the kitchen, she called Eddie and asked him to **come over** because she wanted to see how much he weighed.

Eddie slowly got up and walked to the kitchen. His stomach was empty. There, he stood on the scales, and, to his surprise, he weighed one hundred and sixteen kilogrammes. All the effort, all the food he had eaten, all the amount of water he had drunk, and then, he threw it all up and did not gain any weight. Sarah smiled and said to Eddie that he had a week to slim down to one hundred and eleven kilogrammes.

Eddie sat down on a chair in the kitchen and put his face in his hands. He knew that he was not able to slim down five kilograms in a week. He loved food and did not want to be on a diet.

Eddie stood up, looked at Sarah and asked her if he could see the **to-do list**. The list was long and the whole sheet of paper was full of things that needed to be done in the garden. Eddie closed his eyes and quietly said that he gave up and would do the work in the garden.

Vocabulary

cunning – deceptive; tending to deceive or mislead

bet – the act of gambling
- When one person believes that he can do something, but another person believes that the first person cannot do it, they bet (for whatever they agree on) and then they prove who was right. The one who is right wins; the one who was not right loses.

straight – directly; immediately, without anywhere else

sausage, ham, bacon – products from pork (meat from a pig)

smack lips – to eat noisily

go on a diet – to start a diet in order to lose weight

exercise – the act of moving in order to be fit and lose weight

slim down – to lose weight

sigh – to exhale (breathe out) heavily expressing sadness or tiredness

indicate - to show; to signal

backache – a back pain

hate – to dislike; not like

reduce – to make smaller or less in amount

mow – to cut grass

spruce – to trim (cut) trees in order to make them neat (look good)

bush – a low woody plant with branches; a dense vegetation of stunted trees

chop – to cut

local – relating to a certain location or neighbourhood

pint – A pint is a name for a glass for beer which is the size of a pint. A pint is a unit (about a half a litre).

drink up – to drink until nothing left; to drink the whole amount
– If you drink up your beer, it means that you drink all the beer in the glass (pint) or bottle.
nod – to lower and raise the head to express agreement

curious - interested

weigh – the act of measuring of how heavy something is

achievement – a successful accomplishment

manage – to achieve a goal

mushroom – fungi; soft and porous plant (fungi) that grow from a damp ground (most commonly after rain and usually underneath trees or in woods where the humidity is high and the level of light is low). Some mushrooms are edible but some are not.

hold out a hand – to extend a hand out and forward in order to reach or shake someone else's hand

shook hands - People shake their hands when they clasp each other's right hands to express agreement (or mutual respect).

bath scales – Scales are a device for measuring weigh / how heavy something is. Bath scales are scales for measuring people's weight. (They are called bath scales because they are usually in the bathroom where people usually do not have a carpet and the scales therefore work better)

witness – to see something happen (as a proof)

shout back – to shout at the same person (who shouted first) as a reply

wait and wait – to wait for long (the conjunction 'and' multiplies the meaning of the words it connects)

more and more – increasingly more (the conjunction 'and' multiplies the meaning of the words it connects)

throw up – to vomit; You throw up when you cannot keep something bad in your stomach.

come over – to come somewhere; to visit someone or a place
– If someone comes over to you, they come where you are. If you ask someone to come over, you want them to come to you, to where you are.

to-do list – a list of what needs to be done

A Business Trip

One day, late in the evening, when Albert came home One day, late in the evening, when Albert came home from work, he went **straight** to the bedroom. He did not go to see his wife and say hello to her, and he did not even **get changed**. In the bedroom, he **grabbed** a suitcase, opened it, opened the wardrobe and started packing some clothes.

After some time, Albert's wife, Melania, went to the bedroom to see what his husband was doing there. She watched him for some time, when, eventually, she asked him why he was packing his clothes.

Albert stopped packing, looked up at his wife and quickly said that he was going for a business trip. The business trip **would** last three days, from the following day. He was going to a city very far away. Then, he looked down and quickly continued packing.

When Melania saw that Albert did not get changed and did not even remove his jacket, she asked him why he was so much in a hurry and was packing with his clothes still on when the business trip started the following day.

Albert replied to his wife that he was going to leave that evening because he wanted to drive at night in order to avoid the **traffic**. Then, he explained to his wife that he had a meeting early in the morning, and he would therefore have to get up very early in the morning to drive so far to **make it** to the meeting.

Melania **shrugged her shoulders**, turned around and left the bedroom. She was happy that Albert was going away for three days. They had been arguing a lot recently, and with Albert away, she would at least enjoy her time at home without him.

Albert was happy that Melania did not ask any other questions, and he quickly finished packing. He closed the suitcase, **picked it up**, looked at himself in the mirror, and before he left his **flat**, he shouted at his wife that he was already leaving. Melania said goodbye to him, and Albert closed the door behind him.

Albert sat into his car and drove away. He did not drive far; he just drove a few metres down the road, turned around the corner and parked the car in the **nearby** carpark. He got out of the car and walked back to the **block of flats** where he lived. He opened the **main door** and walked upstairs.

But Albert did not go to the first floor where he lived; he walked to the second floor. He combed his hair and **knocked on the door**. Albert's neighbour, Chloe, who lived in the flat on the second floor opened the door and Albert quickly **went in**.

As soon as Albert went inside the flat, he and Chloe started kissing. During kissing, Albert put down the suitcase, and Chloe removed his jacket. When the jacket fell on the floor, Albert started opening his shirt. Slowly, still kissing, they went to the bedroom.

The next morning, they stayed in bed until noon. Albert made breakfast and coffee, and they both ate and drank it in bed. In the afternoon, Chloe took a bottle of white wine out of the fridge, Albert opened it, and they started drinking.

They sat in a sofa next to each other and drank one glass after another. They soon finished the whole bottle, and Albert opened another one. They drank a lot, and they talked a lot. They laughed about the whole situation of Albert being with Chloe, just one floor above his own flat where his wife was.

They drank more bottles of wine and were slowly getting drunk. As they were getting drunk, they had to remind themselves not to shout too much so that Melania would not hear them. Both Albert and Melania knew that Chloe lived alone. Also, Melania could recognise Albert's voice if he laughed too loudly.

It was already dark outside when Albert and Chloe finished the last bottle of wine. They were both drunk but wanted to drink more. Albert had two bottles of wine in his car, and because it was already dark outside, he decided go to the car and bring the bottles.

Chloe did not like the idea because she was afraid that Melania would see Albert. But Albert knew his wife and was sure that she was already in bed. He slowly got out of the sofa, went to the door, and before he left the flat, he put on his jacket. He put on his jacket because it was cold outside and because he was in pyjamas and did not want to get changed.

Albert slowly opened the door, looked out, and because he did not see and hear anyone in the corridor, he walked out of the flat. Chloe quietly closed the door behind him. Albert was drunk a lot and had to walk very slowly not to fall, especially when he walked on the stairs.

When Albert got to the main door, he pulled out his keys from the pocket of his jacket and unlocked the door. When he closed the door behind him, he locked it.

It was cold outside, but he could not walk fast because he was drunk so much. When he came to the car, he did not even know why went there, but because it was so cold, he sat into the car, closed the door and waited for a while to warm up. Because he was so drunk, Albert **fell asleep**.

Albert woke up in just a few minutes. First, he looked around and did not know what he was doing in his car. Then, he realised that he had come to the car for two bottles of wine he had left there. He found the bottles of wine, took them and left the car. As he walked back to the block of flat, he unlocked the main door, same as **every single time**, and walked slowly upstairs.

Because Albert slept for a few minutes and then woke up still drunk, he was very confused. As he walked upstairs in the block of flats, he did not concentrate and was falling asleep. The only thing he was thinking about was to go to bed and sleep.

When Albert got to the first floor, he opened the door and walked in. It was dark in the hall, but he took off his jacket and threw it on the floor. He walked to the living room, but it was dark in there as well and Chloe was not there. Albert thought that she must have been in bed, so he went to the bedroom.

It was dark in the bedroom as well, and Albert switched on the light. As he switched on the light, he saw his wife in bed with his neighbour from the **ground floor**. Before he **managed** to say anything, he realised that he was in his own flat, not in Chloe's flat, and that he was supposed to be away on a business trip as he had said to his wife.

Instead of being in Chloe's flat, Albert was standing in his own flat, dressed in pyjamas, holding two bottles of wine, and seeing his wife in bed with their neighbour. But before Albert managed to leave the flat, his wife woke up and saw her husband standing in the bedroom next to the bed.

Albert and his wife were staring at each other, not saying anything.

Vocabulary

straight – directly; immediately, without anywhere else

get changed – to change the clothes someone wears

grab – to take or grasp quickly or suddenly

would – the expression of the future time in the context of the past
– The word 'will' is used to express the future time: 'He will do it'. In the past context, you use 'would' instead of 'will': 'He said that he would do it.
The word 'would' is also used to express conditionality or possibility.

traffic – cars moving on a road
- When the traffic is heavy, there are a lot of cars on the roads
- When you want to avoid traffic, you want to drive when the traffic is not heavy

make it – to manage to arrive in time

shrug shoulders

pick up – to take and lift

flat – an apartment

nearby – close; near; not far away (used as an adjective or adverb)

block of flats – a building consisting of a number of flats

main door – the principal / central entrance

knock – to tap or hit loudly enough to be heard when someone wants to attract attention
– You knock on a door when you want someone to open the door.

go in – to walk inside

fall asleep – to start sleeping

every single time – each time without exception or interruption

ground floor – the floor on the ground level

manage – to achieve a goal

A Bald Man's First Girlfriend

It was Friday and after Mark finished work, he went to a bar with his friends to have a few drinks. In the bar, they sat to a large table and ordered beer. Not long after Mark and his friends started drinking, two girls came in and sat at a bar not far from them.

As soon as the girls came to the bar, Mark stopped drinking and **stared** at one of them. The girls were very pretty, but it was one of the girls who Mark liked a lot. The pretty girl who Mark liked did not look happy, and as the girls were talking, Mark listened carefully in order to understand what they were talking about.

It was too noisy in the bar, and Mark did not hear the girls clearly. The only things he could understand were that the pretty girl broke up with her **boyfriend**. He also heard that her boyfriend was bald.

Mark's conclusion was that the pretty girl had broken up with her boyfriend because he was bald. Mark was not happy about it because he was bald as well, but he got an idea. He drank up his beer quickly, hit the table with the empty **pint**, and told his friends that he had an idea.

As soon as Mark finished the last beer, he told his friends that he needed to go and get something at home. Then, he got up and ran out of the bar. Mark did not live far away from the bar and got home in a few minutes.

Before Mark's friends finished their beer, Mark was back in the bar. He opened the door and **walked in**. He walked slowly and confidently, and as he walked towards his friends, he walked closely alongside the bar where the pretty girls sat.

Mark's friends were looking at Mark with their eyes **wide open**. They could not believe what Mark was wearing. At first, they could not even recognise him. Mark was wearing a **wig**.

When mark came to the table where he had sat before with his friends, he ordered a beer and sat down. His friends were looking at him **in puzzlement**, but Mark was smiling.

Mark's friends could not believe that Mark had bought a wig and was wearing it at that moment. None of Mark's friends said a word, but when Mark saw their faces, he explained to them why he had decided to buy a wig.

Mark was getting old and was already bald. But he was still single. And the reason why he believed that he was single was that he was bald. No girl would **go out** with a bald man, Mark thought. Mark had been thinking about buying a wig for some time, and because he was trying to find a girlfriend, he decided to buy one.

That day, when Mark saw a pretty girl in the bar and believed that she was single, he decided to put the wig on and try to ask the girl out. Also, Mark believed that the girl had broken up with her boyfriend because he was bald.

Mark's friends understood and said that he was right. At that moment, though, Mark's friends wanted to see how successful he could be with girls when wearing the wig. Mark was excited and confident and decided to show his friends how a wig could make him successful with women.

Mark stood up, straighten his wig, and slowly walked to the pretty girls who were still sitting at the bar. Mark's friends could not hear what Mark was talking about with the girls, but in a couple of minutes, Mark was walking back to the table where his friends were sitting.

Mark's friends were **astonished** about how confident Mark was and were surprised that the pretty girl Mark liked actually agreed to go out with him. They asked Mark what he was talking about with the girl and what her name was. Her name was Megan.

Mark had arranged a **date** with the girl for the following weekend. His plan was to visit a small village in the **nearby** mountains where he had grown up and sleep over in the local **bed and breakfast**.

On Saturday, Mark got up early in the morning, took a shower, had a shave and put on his best clothes. Then, he put on the wig and carefully arranged it so it looked natural. He looked at himself in the mirror and was satisfied. He could see that he looked younger with the wig **on**. Although Mark was getting old and was already bald, this was the first date in his life.

He did not waste more time looking at himself in the mirror. He put on a clean and shiny pair of shoes and quickly left the house to pick up Megan. On the way to Megan, Mark bought a **bunch of flowers** for her.

When Mark arrived in the place where he and Megan had agreed to meet, she was already waiting for him there. Mark stopped the car, got out, walked around the car, gave Megan the flowers and kissed her **cheek**. Then, he opened the door of his car for her and helped her get in.

The car was clean and looked like new inside. It was the first time Mark had ever cleaned the car, and he had done so because of Megan. He drove slowly, and they talked quietly. When they arrived in the village in the mountains where Mark had grown up, Megan was astonished by the beautiful scenery. She had never been in the mountains before, and she loved it.

First, Mark and Megan went for lunch. They went to eat to a small, old, wooden pub where they sat at a table by a small window so that Megan could see the mountains.

They talked for hours, and the longer they were together, the more Megan liked Mark.

When they finished the lunch, Mark **suggested** that they should go to the nearby bed and breakfast and have a drink there in the bar. Megan agreed and they left the pub. When they arrived in the bed and breakfast, Mark asked for two **single rooms**. Megan was happy to hear that Mark did not plan to sleep in one room with Megan on their first date.

After a few seconds of thinking about it, Megan **interrupted** the man at the reception who was checking if he had two single rooms available and asked him if he had one **double room**. Mark looked at Megan, and when he saw her smile, he smiled as well and agreed. They got one double bedroom in the end.

Before going to the room, Mat and Megan went to the bar and ordered a bottle of wine. But as soon as they sat down, two men came to Mark and said hello to him.

The two men were Mark's old friends who he had grown up with when he lived in the village. Mark had not seen them for years and was surprised to see them in the bar. He stood up, spread his arms and said hello to his old friends. They **hugged** each other and laughed.

Mark showed them that he was there with his girlfriend on their first date and apologised that he could not be with them. They tapped his back, said goodbye and sat at the bar where they ordered beer.

Mark and Megan were **talking and talking**, and when they finished the bottle of wine, Megan felt very tired. Mark paid for the wine and they walked to the room. As Mark walked past his friends, he waved goodbye to them, and his friends waved back at him.

In the room, Megan went to the bathroom to take a shower. Before she went to the shower, she shouted at Mark through the bathroom door saying that she was very tired and instead of a shower, she would prefer to take a bath. Megan also said to Mark that she wanted to be in the bath for long in order to relax. In the meantime, Megan said, Mark could go **downstairs** to the bar and meet and talk to his friends he had met.

Mark was actually happy to hear that. He wanted to go and have a chat with his old friends. He said that it was a great idea and agreed. He promised to be back soon, but Megan replied that he did not have to worry about time and should enjoy the time with his old friends. She wanted to enjoy the bath for a very long time.

Mark left the room and ran downstairs to the bar. There, he met his old friends, hugged them again and ordered **gin and tonic**. Mark's friends asked Mark about him a lot of questions. They wanted to know how his life had changed since he moved out of the village, and they were also surprised that he had a girlfriend because he had never **been in a relationship** before. Mark smiled and said a little **shyly** that the girl was his first girlfriend and repeated that that day was their first date.

When Mark's friends heard that, they wanted to celebrate it. Mark **shook his head** and said that Megan was taking a bath, and he had promised to her to come back soon. Mark's friends laughed and ordered another glass of gin and tonic for him. Mark knew that Megan wanted to enjoy her bath for a long time, so he **reluctantly** accepted another drink and stayed in the bar.

Mark and his friends had a good time. They had not seen each other for a long time, and they talked about their **youth**, their growing up and their **current** lives. Mark's friends asked him how he had met his new girlfriend and why he had never had a girlfriend before. Mark was very keen on telling them everything.

Mark ordered another glass of gin and tonic and started explaining to his friends that he had been unsuccessful with women because he was bald. Then, Mark told them about the wig he had bought and as soon as he had put it on and asked Megan out, she had agreed. Then, Mark described to his friends the whole situation when he had first put the wig on in a pub and how amazed his friends were when he asked Megan for a date and she had agreed.

As Mark was telling his friends how he had met Megan, he and his friends drank a few more drinks. When Mark finished the story about the wig, his friends laughed, and Mark laughed with them. But his friends did not believe him. They said to him that it was a good story, especially the part when he said that he was bald and was wearing a wig. Mark stopped laughing and looked at his friends. Then, he **grabbed** his wig and pulled it down.

Mark's friends stopped laughing immediately and were looking at him with their mouths open. They could not believe that Mark was really bald and was wearing a wig. Mark put the wig back on his head and ordered another glass of gin and tonic. Mark's friends ordered drinks as well, and they all started talking and laughing again.

Because Mark was drinking so much, he **lost a track of time** and did not realise that Megan was waiting for him upstairs in the room. Megan was very tired and as she lay in the bath, she was getting sleepy. She got out of the bath, dried herself and went to the bedroom.

Mark was not back from the bar yet, and Megan decided to wait for him in bed. She covered herself with a blanket and started reading a book. She did not want to go to the bar because she believed that Mark enjoyed talking to his friends, and she did not want to interfere.

As Megan waited for Mark in bed, she finally **fell asleep**. In the meantime, Mark was still sitting in the bar, drinking. The more drunk Mark was, the less he thought about Megan and the time, and he did not realise how late it was. In the end, Mark got drunk so much that he fell asleep at the bar. His friends were drunk as well and decided to go home. They woke Mark up and left.

Mark got up and slowly walked out of the bar. As he walked upstairs to his room, his head was **itchy** from having worn the wig all day. He removed the wig and scratched his bald head. Because he was drunk and did not concentrate, he did not put the wig back on his head and held it in his hand.

When Mark walked in his room, Megan was already **fast asleep**. He did not want to wake her up, but because he was drunk, he suddenly lost his balance and fell on the floor. As he fell, Megan woke up.

It was dark in the room, but the moon was shining and a little bit of the moonlight shone into the room through the window. Mark slowly got up from the floor, and because he was next to Megan's bed, Megan could see him when he got up. But Megan could not **tell** that it was Mark. What she saw was a man without hair who was moving from side to side, **mumbling** something **unintelligible**.

Megan thought that it was a **robber** who moved from side to side because he was panicking when she had woken up. She also thought that he was mumbling because he was quickly talking to himself, trying to think about what to do and how to run away.

Megan did not wait. She jumped out of the bed and ran outside the room. She was in her pyjamas, but she did not care. She was scared and ran as fast as she could. When Megan got downstairs, she went to the reception and **reported** the robber in her room.

Mark was shocked to see Megan running away from the room so scared, and he **sobered up** a little. He thought about what to do, but when he realised that he held his wig in his hand, he understood what had happened. Because Mark did not want Megan to see him so drunk, and because he did not want her to know that he was bald, he decided to run away.

He knew that he could not leave through the door and run by the reception, so he decided to escape through the window. It was very dangerous, especially because he was so drunk, but he **managed** to **climb down** and run away.

Mark ran to his car and drove away from the bed and breakfast carpark. He did not want Megan to find him there in the morning, so he drove the car about a mile away and parked it in the woods. As soon as he switched the car off, he fell asleep.

Megan and the receptionist went to the room to see if the robber was still there. He was not there anymore, but they noticed that the window in the room was open. Their conclusion was that the robber must have got to the room through the window and then escape through it as well because no stranger had walked through the reception.

The receptionist called the police, and when the police arrived, Megan tried to describe the person to them. She talked about an old, ugly and bald man who was moving very slowly, seemed **unstable** and had a deep voice. He did not say anything but was mumbling something she could not understand. The police wrote down the description and left.

When Mark woke up, he first did not know where he was. He woke up in his car in the middle of the woods. He soon realised that he had got drunk the previous night. He was hungover and had a headache.

He drove back to the bed and breakfast and parked the car. Then, he put on the wig and went to the bed and breakfast. The receptionist told him, though, that Megan had been already gone, and no one knew where she was.

Mark had never seen Megan again.

Vocabulary

bald – without hair

girlfriend – a girl or woman who is in a relationship with a man

stare – to look with fixed eyes; to look constantly with eyes wide open

boyfriend – a man who is in a relationship with a woman

pint – a capacity measure (about half a litre); a name for a standard size of a glass of beer

walk in – to go inside

wide open – fully open

wig – artificial hair

in puzzlement - confusedly

go out (with someone) – to go on a date; to meet someone as a potential partner

astonished – surprised; amazed; stunned

date – a meeting arranged in advance, usually with a potential partner

nearby – close; near; not far away (used as an adjective or adverb)

bed and breakfast – a boarding house (similar to a hotel) where you can sleep and have breakfast

on – wearing
- When you have something on (clothes, jewellery, wig…), it means that you wear it (you have in on your body)

bunch of flowers – a number of flowers together

cheek – the side part of a face

suggest – to make a proposal; to express an idea

single room – a room in a hotel for one person

interrupt – to stop and disrupt someone's speech suddenly

double room – a room in a hotel for two people

hug – to squeeze someone in hands to show love or affection

talk and talk – to talk a lot (the conjunction 'and' multiplies the meaning of the words it connects)

downstairs – in the lower floor

gin and tonic – a drink mixed with gin (an alcoholic beverage) and tonic

be in a relationship – to have a partner

shyly – in a timid manner; timidly; not boldly or courageously

shake someone's head – When you shake your head, you express disagreement by moving your head from left to right.

reluctantly – not willingly

youth – when young; the early period

current – at the moment; present-day; today's

as – while; during the time when

grab – to take or grasp quickly or suddenly

lose track of time – to lose the grasp / awareness of what the time is

fall asleep – to start sleeping

itchy – When your skin is itchy, you have a need to scratch it.

fast asleep – to be sleeping deeply

tell – to recognise; to recognise the difference; to be able to discern / distinguish / differentiate; to identify

mumble – to speak indistinctly / unintelligibly

unintelligible – not clear; indistinct

robber – a person who comes into someone's house in order to steal things

report – to inform; the act of informing; to make known to the authorities

sober up – to become sober; not to be drunk anymore

manage – to achieve a goal

climb down – to get down / lower height with a slow, gradual progress

unstable – not balanced; unable to stay without falling

Two Fishermen and Their Lonely Wives

Joe and Amanda wanted to get married, but they did not know how to say that to Amanda's father. Amanda's father, Larry, liked the **outdoors**. He liked **hiking**, cycling, **camping**, **mushrooming**, **canoeing**, and horse riding. What he liked most was **fishing**.

Joe, on the other hand, liked being at home, playing computer games. He did not like walking or cycling, and every time he needed to go somewhere, he drove or took a bus or different **public transport**.

Joe did not like wasting time, and every time he had a free moment, he played games on his phone. He played games when he was on the bus, on the train, when he was queueing and sometimes even when he was walking on the street.

Amanda was complaining to Joe that he spent all his free time at home and played computer games. She often wanted to go out with him, to go for a walk, to sit in the park or to go cycling. But Joe never wanted. He enjoyed playing computer games more than spending his time outside.

Amanda hoped that if they got married, Joe would spend less time playing computer games and spend more time with her. Amanda and Joe's plan was to move to Amanda's cottage after their marriage. The cottage was old and needed a lot of **refurbishment**, but Amanda did not mind and was looking forward to working on her new house with Joe. Like this, they **would** also have a chance to spend more time together.

Joe liked the idea of moving to her father's **cottage** as well because at that moment, Joe and Amanda could not afford to buy their own house and were **renting** a small flat.

Both Amanda and Joe knew that Larry, Amanda's father, did not like Joe very much. Joe did not know why exactly, but Amanda was saying to him that it was because he liked playing computer games, which her father thought was wasting time. Also, Larry did not like that Joe did not do anything else and did not even go outside. He was always sitting at home.

Amanda and Joe were thinking how and when to tell Larry that they wanted to get married. They were afraid that Larry would not agree with their marriage because he did not like Joe and would not want his daughter to marry him.

Joe and Larry needed to become friends. Larry needed to like Joe before Joe would ask him to marry his daughter. But how could they make Larry like Joe when they were so different?

While Joe was **busy** playing computer games, Amanda was lying in bed, thinking. She **thought and thought**, when she suddenly got an idea.

Amanda quickly **sat up**, turned towards Joe and shouted that she had got an idea. Joe did not want to stop playing, so he only asked what idea she had got and **kept** playing. Amanda quickly got up and ran to Joe. She **grabbed** his shoulders, asked him to stop playing and listen to her.

Joe was surprised that Amanda wanted to talk to him so urgently, so he stopped playing and switched off the computer. Then, he turned towards her and listened to what Amanda had to say to him.

Amanda sat back on a bed and quietly told Joe that if he pretended to like some of her father's hobbies, her father would like him. Joe did not like the idea and shook his head. But then he got up and thought about it for a while. He walked around the room and counted on his fingers all hobbies Larry had and all the things Larry liked doing.

First, he mentioned hiking. Hiking, he said, was not a real hobby, and he also believed that even if he liked hiking, it would not make Larry like him. Then, cycling and canoeing. These, he believed, were the same as hiking, and Larry would not suddenly like Joe just because of him liking cycling and canoeing. Then, Joe thought about mushrooming, but he could not pretend to like mushrooming because he did not like mushrooms, and he could not even **tell edible** mushrooms from poisonous mushrooms. Also, Larry already knew that Joe did not like mushrooms.

But then, Amanda shouted: Fishing! Joe was quickly **shaking his head**, but Amanda **insisted** that it was a great idea. If Joe said to Larry that he liked fishing or that he would like to learn it, Larry would be happy to hear that and would like him immediately. Larry liked everyone who liked fishing, and people who he was going fishing with sooner or later always became his best friends.

Joe did not like the idea, but Amanda kept saying that it was the only way for her father to like him and to agree with their marriage. The whole evening, Amanda was begging Joe to tell her father that he liked fishing until Joe eventually agreed.

Amanda was so happy that Joe had agreed that she hugged him and danced with him in the room. Joe was happy that Amanda was happy, but he was still not sure if it really was a good idea to pretend and lie to Amanda's father that he liked fishing.

The problem with the idea was that Joe had never **gone fishing** before and did not know anything about fishing. When Joe said that to Amanda, Amanda replied to him that it did not matter because her father had never talked a lot about fishing with anyone, so he would not be asking Joe many questions and would not find out that Joe actually did not know anything about fishing.

When Amanda told Joe that her father was not talking about fishing with other people, Joe was a little relieved, and again, he agreed to tell Larry and pretend that he liked fishing. Amanda was very happy, thanked Joe and hugged him again.

Amanda and Joe planned to invite Larry for dinner, and at that moment, Joe would tell him that he liked fishing. Then, after **befriending** Larry, Joe would tell him that he would like to marry Amanda.

*

Amanda and Joe **arranged** a dinner with Larry for the following Saturday. Amanda was very excited, but Joe was nervous. Amanda cooked her father's favourite food, and Joe bought a bottle of wine, hoping that they would all celebrate after Joe telling Larry that he would like to marry Amanda.

Larry arrived in Amanda and Joe's house at the time they had agreed. Joe welcomed Larry, and they sat down to the dining table. Joe opened the bottle of wine he had bought, and as they both drank, they talked.

Amanda was ready to **serve** dinner, but when she saw Joe talking with her father, she waited with the dinner in order to give Joe more time to tell Larry that he liked fishing. Amanda could not hear from the kitchen what Joe and Larry talked about in the dining room, but she believed Joe would tell Larry as soon as possible to **get it over with**.

After a few moments, Amanda heard Joe and Larry laughing. She believed that Joe had told Larry at that moment about fishing, and she started serving dinner. As she served dinner to them, she asked what they were talking about, expecting to hear from her father about Joe's new hobby. But both Joe and Larry just waved their hands and said that they had talked about the past.

When Amanda sat to the table next to Joe and Larry, she poured herself a glass of wine and looked at Joe. Joe looked at Amanda and knew that she wanted to know if he had already told Larry about him liking fishing. Joe looked down and **shook his head**, indicating to Amanda that he had not told her father yet.

Larry was pleased to see that Amanda cooked his favourite meal, and as soon as Amanda sat down, he started eating. When Amanda saw that her father was happy about the meal, she smiled at Joe and nodded at him, giving him a sign that it was a good time to tell her father about fishing.

Joe took a deep breath and said to Larry that he liked fishing. Amanda looked at Joe and smiled at him. But suddenly, Larry stopped eating, looked at Joe and asked if it was true. Joe **shrugged his shoulders**, nodded and said that it was true.

Larry did not talk about fishing and just asked Joe where he was usually going fishing. Joe quickly answered that he had not found a good place yet where he would be going regularly and said that he was usually fishing in the **nearby** river in different places.

Larry nodded, smiled at Joe, and was very happy that Joe liked fishing. Amanda could see that her father was happy and liked Joe a bit more. After they finished dinner, Larry patted Joe on the back, and Amanda poured them both another glass of wine. Then, Amanda said to her father that Joe had something to tell him. She looked at Joe, and Joe stood up and said to Larry that he would like to marry Amanda.

When Larry heard that, he had a drink of wine, stood up and said to Joe that he would agree with him marrying his daughter only if he was a good fisherman. Joe was shocked and looked at Larry with his mouth open.

Larry smiled at both Joe and Amanda, thanked them for the dinner and walked towards the door in order to leave the house. Before Larry left the house, Joe said to him that he was a good fisherman. But Larry did not say anything. He just turned around, looked at Joe, smiled at him, said goodbye and left.

Joe was puzzled, but Amanda just shrugged her shoulders and said that her father was joking and probably just wanted to think about their marriage. But Amanda was happy. She knew that Larry liked Joe when Joe had told him that he liked fishing, and she believed that her father would have agreed with their marriage. Joe was also happy because Larry did not talk about fishing with him, and he therefore did not find out that Joe actually did not know anything about fishing.

It was Saturday, and Amanda and Joe **stood up** late. Amanda was reading a book, and Joe was playing a computer game. They did not talk about the dinner with Larry, and Joe hoped that he would never have to talk about fishing with Larry.

*

The next day, very early in the morning, someone rang the doorbell at Amanda and Joe's house. Amanda and Joe were still in bed and **fast asleep**. The doorbell rang for the second time, but both Amanda and Joe did not wake up. Amanda woke up only when the doorbell rang for the third time.

When the doorbell rang for the fourth time, Joe still did not wake up. Amanda took Joe's shoulder and shook him gently. Joe woke up, complained and asked Amanda why she had woken him up. But before Amanda answered, the doorbell rang again.

Joe got up, and as he walked towards the door, he complained about who was ringing the doorbell so early. Joe opened the door and saw that it was Larry.

Larry said good morning to Joe and smiled at him. It was still dark outside, but when Larry walked inside Joe's house, Joe saw that Larry was wearing **camouflage suit** and **wellington boots** and carried **fishing tackle**.

Joe could see that Larry was going fishing but did not understand why he had woken him up. Before Joe **managed** to ask Larry why he had **come around** so early, Larry asked Joe to quickly put on his fishing clothes and go fishing with him.

Joe was still half asleep, but when he heard that, he woke up immediately. Joe could not believe that Larry wanted Joe to go fishing with him. Joe was shocked. He **stood still** in front of Larry and thought about what to say.

When Larry saw Joe standing in front of him and looking at him in shock, he told him to harry up because the best time for fishing was at **daybreak**. Joe was still standing still, but when he heard Amanda shouting at him from the bedroom, asking who had rung the doorbell, Joe turned around and went to the bedroom.

In the bedroom, Joe told Amanda that it was her father who had rung the doorbell. Amanda **sat up** and asked why he had come around and what he wanted. Joe was shaking and answered that Larry wanted him to go fishing with him.

Amanda was shocked to hear that and remembered what her father had said the previous day after dinner. Her father had said that he would agree with their wedding only if Joe was a good fisherman. That morning, Larry came over to ask Joe to go fishing with him in order to find out if he was a good fisherman.

Joe started shaking even more, but he had to go. He put on some old clothes which he thought were the most appropriate for fishing and went to see Larry. Larry asked Joe if those were his fishing clothes, but Joe made and excuse and said that he was not usually going fishing too often and was **saving up** for **proper** fishing clothes.

Larry smiled, but later he nodded and said that it was OK. They sat on their bikes and cycled to the nearby river. Larry took Joe to his favourite spot where he gave him one of his fishing rods. Then, Larry **unfolded** two fishing chairs, set up his fishing rod, put a **bait** on the fish hook, **cast the line** and sat down.

Joe watched Larry attentively and did everything exactly the same way as Larry. Joe was shaking and was very **clumsy**, but Larry did not watch him. After Joe managed to put a bait on the fish hook and cast the line, he sat down next to Larry.

Larry was not talking, and Joe felt **awkward**. After some time, Joe thought that it was not appropriate to sit next to Larry without saying anything, so he asked him how long he had been going fishing.

Larry did not answer. Instead, he turned towards Joe and put his finger on his lips to show him that he should not speak. Joe **found** it very boring and was thinking about how long Larry wanted to be there. Then, Larry quietly said that fishing was not about talking. Talking and **chatting** could be done in a pub. Fishing, on the other hand, was about appreciating the silence and listening to the river, to the wind and to the birds singing.

Joe did not understand what Larry was talking about. How could anyone enjoy listening to the river, the wind or to the birds, he though. He thought that fishing was about catching a fish as soon as possible and take it home.

The only noise that Joe had ever focused on before was the sound in the computer games he played. But because Joe had nothing to do while he was sitting by the river, he closed his eyes and listen to all the sounds around him. He found the sound of the wind, the river and the birds very **soothing** and felt very relaxed.

Larry was **sitting still** for quite a long time when he suddenly stood up and took two sandwiches and a flask with warm coffee. He sat back on his chair and gave one sandwich to Joe. Then, Larry poured two cups of coffee, one for himself and one for Joe and started talking to Joe. They were sitting close to each other and talked quietly.

Larry did not talk about fishing; he talked about Joe and Amanda. He asked Joe about how they had met and what their plans for the future were. As Joe and Larry ate and talked, they also laughed.

Joe had always thought that Larry was a **grumpy** man, but that day when they were fishing together, Joe realised that Larry was actually a very good and friendly man.

Joe and Larry were fishing the whole day, but they did not catch any fish. Late in the evening, when Joe came home, he was tired but **mentally** relaxed. He had not felt like that before. In fact, the computer games he had played usually made him stressed, and he always found it difficult to **fall asleep** in the evenings.

Joe took a shower and went straight to bed. Amanda wanted to talk to him about his day with Larry, but as soon as Joe lay in bed, he fell asleep. Amanda was surprised because she had never seen Joe fall asleep so quickly.

The next day, when Joe went to work, he was thinking about the previous day he had spent with Larry. For some reason, Joe was missing the peaceful silence and the sound of the river and birds. He realised that he had never spent a day in the **countryside**. Instead, he had spent every day playing games on his computer.

When Joe went home from work, he was stressed. He was stressed from work and from the **traffic**. But when he was arriving home, he saw Larry's bike in front of his house. Joe went in and saw Larry in his camouflage suit and wellington boots, carrying all his fishing tackle.

Joe and Larry **greeted** each other, and they hugged. Larry said to Joe that the previous day they had not caught any fish, so they should try again. Joe smiled and said to Larry to wait a moment for him to get changed.

Joe ran into the bedroom to get changed in order to go fishing with Larry. Amanda was surprised that Joe wanted to go fishing with Larry again, but before she even had a chance to talk to Joe, he was already leaving, saying goodbye to her and giving her a kiss.

The door closed and the house was suddenly quiet. Amanda was alone again. Being at home alone, Amanda felt lonely. Joe on the other hand did not feel lonely. When he was with Larry, he felt like he was with his best friend.

Joe and Larry arrived in the same place where they had been the previous day. They unfolded their chairs, set up their fishing rods, put a bait on the fish hook, cast the line and sat down. Joe asked if Larry took some beer. Larry looked at Joe, **winked** at him, got up and took two bottles of cold beer out of his bag.

They talked quietly again. Joe told Larry about how much he had enjoyed fishing with him the previous day, how much he had liked the quietness by the river and how relaxed he had been when he came home. Larry smiled and nodded.

Suddenly, Joe's **float** sank and the **spinning reel** started **unwinding**. That meant only one thing – a fish **bit** Joe's fish hook! Joe shouted and jumped up. He was very excited but did not know what to do. He shouted at Larry, asking what to do, and Larry shouted back at Joe, giving him instructions, telling him what to do.

Joe was panicking and was constantly shouting at Larry asking what to do, what to do next and how to do it. Without helping Joe, Larry still stayed behind Joe, smiled and kept telling Joe what to do. For Larry, it was just a fish. But for Joe, it was the most exciting thing that had happened to him in a long time. He was catching a fish! A real fish! It was **nothing like** a computer game. This was real.

Joe and Larry managed to pull the fish out of the river, and Joe held it in his hands. It was a large fish, and Joe was excited and was laughing. Larry filled a **bucket** with water, and they put the fish in the bucket. The fish was so large that it took the whole space in the bucket. Joe felt very proud.

But they did not go home right after catching the fish. They sat down on their small chairs, with Joe's bait back in the river. They did not catch another fish that day, but after catching one, Joe was happy and excited for the rest of the day. Both Joe and Larry enjoyed sitting at the **bank** of the river so much that they decided to go home only when it was already dark.

Same as the previous day, Joe was tired when he came home. Because it was late, Amanda was already in bed. When Joe went to bed, Amanda wanted to talk to him.

But Joe was so tired that as soon as he lay down in bed, he fell asleep.

The next day, Larry had to stay longer at work and could not go fishing with Joe. Joe was unhappy about it. He did not have his own fishing tackle and could not go fishing on his own. That day, after he came home from work, Joe decided to go and buy his own fishing tackle.

When Joe came home from work, Amanda ran to him and hugged him. She told him how much she missed him and **begged** him not to go fishing with Larry that day because she wanted to be with him.

Joe smiled at Amanda and said to her that Larry had to stay at work longer so they could not go fishing that day. But Joe also said to her that he wanted to go and buy his own fishing tackle. Amanda was happy and wanted to go shopping with Joe. She was happy that she could be with Joe that day.

That day, when Joe and Amanda were shopping, Amanda was surprised to find out that Joe had not been going fishing with Larry because of Larry, but because he himself had enjoyed it.

Joe was telling Amanda what it was like to go fishing. He talked about the **tranquillity**, and what it was like to be on his own or just with a friend, with no other people around, with no noise, no traffic and no stress.

Joe also talked about the soothing sound of the river and the wind, he talked about how relaxing it was to listen to bird singing, and he talked about how refreshing at the same time it all was.

Amanda was very surprised to hear that. The way she knew Joe was that he liked to play computer games and doing nothing else. She had always thought that Joe believed that sitting by a river was boring and that it was a waste of time. She shrugged her shoulders but was happy that he liked Larry and that Larry liked him.

*

The next day, when Joe came back home from work, he saw Larry's bicycle in front of his house again. He smiled and quickly went in. Joe was looking forward to showing Larry his new fishing tackle he had bought the previous day.

But when Joe walked inside the house, he saw Larry and Amanda sitting at the dinner table. Joe walked toward them, said hello to them, kissed Amanda and shook his hand with Larry. Larry was not wearing his fishing clothes and did not have his fishing tackle with him.

Amanda was ready to serve a meal and asked Joe to sit down. Larry said to Joe that he wanted to talk to them. Joe thought that something bad had happened, but before they started to eat, Larry said to Joe and Amanda that he would be happy if they got married.

Both Joe and Amanda started jumping up and down, they were hugging and kissing each other, and then, they were hugging Larry. When Joe and Amanda calmed down a little, Larry said that Joe was a good fisherman, that he had caught a fish faster than him and that he would be happy if Amanda married such a great fisherman.

They all laughed and started eating. After dinner, Joe showed Larry his new fishing tackle, and they both spent the rest of the day talking about nothing else but fishing. The next day, Joe said to Larry that he wanted to buy some proper camouflage suit and wellington boots. Larry recommended Joe that he should also buy a hat so that they could go fishing in bad weather as well.

*

Joe and Amanda had their wedding in a month. They invited all **members** of their families; they ate, they drank and they danced. But Joe spent most of the time with Larry and talked about fishing.

Amanda and Joe took a **week off** after their wedding. Because they were saving money for repairing a cottage they had got from Amanda's parents, they did not go on **honeymoon**. Instead, they wanted to stay at home and enjoy being together as husband and wife.

The day after Amanda and Joe's wedding, Amanda woke up and **stretched** her arms. As Amanda was stretching her arms, she noticed that Joe was not sleeping next to her. She opened her eyes, switched the light on and quickly looked next to her in bed. Joe was not there.

Amanda sat up in bed and called Joe's name. There was no answer. She got up and went to the bathroom, but Joe was not there. She called Joe's name again, but again, there was no answer. Joe was not at home.

Amanda thought that Joe went to a shop to buy some nice food so he could make nice breakfast. She went back to the bedroom and went back to bed because she was very tired from the wedding from the previous day. But before she switched off the light, she noticed a note written on a sheet of paper on Joe's bedside table.

She slowly **reached** for the sheet of paper and read the note. In the note, Joe explained to Amanda that he went fishing with Larry and promised to be back home soon.

Amanda quietly complained because she wanted to spend the whole day with Joe. But hoping that Joe would be back soon, she switched off the light and fell asleep.

When Amanda woke up, it was already noon, but Joe was still not at home. She got up, walked around the house to see if Joe was at home or not, and when she found out that Joe was still fishing, she made breakfast for herself, sat into a sofa and watched TV.

It was the first day after her wedding, and Amanda was at home alone while Joe was fishing. She did not think that she would be alone after her wedding day and felt sad. Amanda finished her breakfast, and instead of waiting for Joe at home, she wrote a note to him, explaining that she went to visit her mother.

When Amanda visited her mother, she complained to her that Joe was spending too much time fishing with her father. He was going fishing almost every day and was coming home late at night. At the weekends, Joe was going fishing early in the morning, and was coming home at night. It was the weekends when Amanda felt lonely most.

First, Amanda had been complaining to her mum that Joe had been spending all his free time playing computer games and that he had never wanted to go out. And then, after being married, Amanda was complaining that Joe was always out, spending all his free time fishing, and was never at home. Amanda also complained to her mum about feeling very lonely.

Amanda's mother replied to Amanda that she had the same life because her husband, Larry, was going fishing almost every day and was coming home at night. If she wanted to be with her husband, Amanda's mum told her, she had to go fishing with him.

Amanda thought that it was a good idea, and the next day when Joe and Larry went fishing, she went with them. Joe and Larry were not going to the river so often any more. They preferred fishing from a boat in a large lake that was located not far from the town where they lived.

Joe had a boat which he had got from Larry as a wedding present, and they both used the boat for fishing. They always paddled to the middle of the lake and were fishing there. They used to say to their wives that it was even more peaceful there in the middle of the lake than at the bank of the river. They were also catching more fish in the lake.

Amanda did not enjoy going fishing with Joe and Larry because they always spent the whole day in the little boat and did not talk much. And when they talked, it was only about fishing.

Instead of going fishing with Joe and Larry, Amanda spent her time at home. Because she was always alone and was always bored, she started playing computer games. At first, she did not enjoy them, but later, she found some games that she liked. She played often and the better she was at playing the games, the more she enjoyed them.

Not long after Amanda started playing computer games, she was playing computer games every day until late at night – until her husband Joe came home from fishing.

Vocabulary

fisherman – a person who catches fish (as a profession or hobby)

lonely – separated from other people
- If you are alone but wish to be with other people, you feel lonely.

outdoors – the area outside (outside the house) in the countryside

hike – to walk a long way for pleasure or exercise

camp – to live for a time in a tent on holiday

mushrooming – the act of picking mushrooms

canoeing – the activity of paddling a canoe (a light, narrow boat)

fishing – the act of catching fish

public transport – transport such as buses and trains that transport the public (people) from place to place

refurbishment – the renovation of a building

would – the expression of the future time in the context of the past
– The word 'will' is used to express the future time: 'He will do it'. In the past context, you use 'would' instead of 'will': 'He said that he would do it.
The word 'would' is also used to express conditionality or possibility.

cottage – a small house, usually in the country (not a city)

rent – to pay someone for the use of a property

busy – occupied

thought and thought – to think a lot (the conjunction 'and' multiplies the meaning of the words it connects)

sit up – You sit up from the position of lying.
– When you sit up in bed, it means that you are lying and then you sit up (you are not lying anymore).

keep (doing something) – to continue (doing something)

grab – to take or grasp quickly or suddenly

tell – distinguish; to recognise the difference

edible – suitable to eat

get something over with – to finish something

shake someone's head – When you shake your head, you express disagreement by moving your head from left to right.

insist – to assert to be true

go fishing – to go out to catch fish; to practise the hobby of fishing

befriend – to become friends

arrange – to organise

serve – to present (food or drink) to someone

shrug someone's shoulders – When you shrug your shoulders, you lift them up to express certain thoughts or feelings according to the context (for example indifference, disinterest, unconcern, the lack of knowledge, and so on).

nearby – close; near; not far away (used as an adjective or adverb)

stay up – to be awake and not to go to bed

mentally – involving or relating to the mind

fast asleep – sleeping deeply

camouflage suit – a suit with the colour of the fabric suitable / appropriate to fit into the surrounding area in the countryside

wellington boots – tall rubber boots

fishing tackle – an equipment used for fishing

manage – to achieve; to make possible

come around – to come to someone's house for a visit

stand still – to stand without moving

daybreak – the first light of day

sit up – You sit up from the position of lying.
– When you sit up in bed, it means that you are lying and then you sit up (you are not lying anymore).

save up – to save enough money for something

proper – good enough; appropriate and good quality

unfold – to open what is folded (closed in order to be smaller)

bait – something used to lure; anything that serves as an enticement (in order to attract)

cast the line – You cast the line when you throw a fishing hook with a bait into the water to catch a fish.

clumsy – showing lack of skills

awkward – uneasy; not at ease socially; unsure

find (in this case) – to perceive

chat – an informal conversation

soothe – to give moral or emotional strength in order to make feel better

sit still – to sit without moving

grumpy – bad-tempered and sulky; who is never happy and always complains

fall asleep – to start sleeping

countryside – the natural and rural region outside towns and cities.

traffic – cars moving on a road
- When the traffic is heavy, there are a lot of cars on the roads
- When you want to avoid traffic, you want to drive when the traffic is not heavy

greet – to say hello or goodbye

wink – to close one eye quickly as a signal

float – something that remains / floats on the surface of water (when it sinks, it indicates that a fish bit and pulled the fishing hook down)

spinning reel – a device on a fishing rod on which a fishing line is wound / coiled up.

unwind – to uncoil
- When a fish bites onto a fishing hook and pulls it down, it unwinds the fishing line which is wound up on the spinning wheel.

nothing like – far from; a long way from; nowhere near; not as good as

bucket – a cylindrical vessel open at the top. When a fisherman catches a fish, it fills a bucket with water and puts the fish in it.

bank – the land alongside the edge of a river

beg – to ask humbly, eagerly and earnestly; to plead; to implore

tranquillity – the quality of state of being very calm

member – A member of a family is the person who forms the family.

week off – a week without work (professional work); a week when a person does not have to go to work

honeymoon – a holiday taken by a newly married couple

stretch – to straighten and prolong (for example muscles in order to wake up better)

reach – to extend as far as

A Dating Advert Gone Wrong

Al was a young man. His name was actually Alfred, but everyone called him Al. He was a college student and lived in the **halls of residence**. Al shared his room with his friend Gary, who studied in the same college as Al.

Al was a very good student because he studied every day, even at the weekends. But the reason why he studied every day was that he did not have any hobby and was **single**. He was **going out** sometimes with his friends, but because he was very **shy**, he had never talked to any girl he liked.

Al did not want to be single and wanted to find a **girlfriend**. Because he was too shy to approach women in order to talk to them, he could not get a **date**, which made him very sad.

One day, late in the evening, when Al was lying in his bed and studied from **textbooks**, his friend Gary was sitting in an armchair next to Al and read a newspaper. Suddenly, Gary **put down** the newspaper and said to Al that he had an idea of how Al could find a girlfriend.

Al stopped reading the textbook he had studied from and looked at Gary, interested in what idea Gary had. Gary stood up and put the newspaper he had read on top of

Al's textbooks. Then, he pointed at a page he wanted Al to read.

There were adverts on the whole page, but Al did not read them. He did not understand why Gary wanted him to read the adverts and asked him about it. Gary smiled, turned around and went back to his armchair. He sat down in the armchair and told Al to read them.

Al started reading the adverts and quickly realised that they were dating adverts. He looked at Gary with his mouth open. He understood; he could get a date with a girl by replying to some of the adverts. Gary was smiling at Al, and Al smiled back at Gary.

Al **sat up** in his bed and started reading the adverts. To his **disappointment**, he did not like any of them because the girls who were advertising were very **demanding** about what they expected from the partners they were looking for.

Also, a lot of girls in the adverts wrote about how pretty they were, and Al believed that they were lying about themselves. After Al read a few adverts, the next advert **caught his eye**.

Al read the advert **out loud** so Gary could hear it. The advert was **posted** by a girl who wrote that she was very pretty and was looking for a rich man. Both Al and Gary laughed and **shook their heads**. They did not understand who would ever reply to an advert like that.

Al and Gary talked about the advert for a while and wandered what kind of girl might have written it and if she was really pretty. As they talked about it, they decided to try an **experiment**.

The experiment Al and Gary decided to try was to reply to the advert and pretend that they were a rich man. Neither Al nor Gary wanted to go on the date with the girl, though, because they believed that she was lying about herself and they would find it awkward to meet her.

Instead of them going, they thought about asking one of their friends to go and meet the girl. First, they did not know which of their friends they could send, but after a few moments of thinking, they thought about Hank.

Hank was not Al and Gary's friend, but he was Gary's older brother's friend, and both Gary and Hank knew each other well. Also, Hank was single and lived alone. Al and Gary wanted Hank to **go on a date** with the girl because they expected that the girl, who was looking for a rich man, would want the man to spend a lot of money on her. What is more, Hank lived in the city, same as rich people, so Al and Gary could use Hank's address where the girl from the advert could reply to.

On Saturday, Al and Gary went to the city and visited Hank. Hank invited them **in**, made some tea for everyone, and when they all sat down, Hank asked them why they had come to visit him. When Al and Gary told Hank the reason of their visit, Hank thought that they were joking. Hank asked them what the point would be to go on a date with the girl when the girl was looking for someone rich. And, Hank was not rich.

Al and Gary **kept** convincing Hank that it would be interesting to see what the girl was like. Then, they offered Hank some money so, if the girl really came to the date, Hank could enjoy the time with her. In the end, Hank agreed, but added that Al and Gary were wasting their money and Hank was wasting his time. Hank did not believe that the girl would come, and if she did, she would not want to spend her time with him because she would soon find out that Hank was not rich. But he shrugged his shoulders and, again, said that he agreed.

As soon as Al and Gary came back to their room, Al started writing a letter in which he explained that he was very rich and was looking to meet a pretty girl. Then, he explained that he had found her advert in a newspaper and would love to meet her. At the end of the letter, Al wrote that he was rich. As Al was writing the letter, both he and Gary laughed.

The next day, after Al finished school, he went to the post office and posted the letter. When he came back to his room in the halls of residence and told Gary that the letter had been posted, they both laughed and wondered whether or not the girl would reply.

Time passed, one day after another, but Al and Gary did not hear from Hank whether he had received any reply from the girl. When two weeks passed, they were slowly forgetting about it all and believed that the girl was not interested.

One day, on Monday afternoon, Hank waited for Al and Gary in front of the college where they studied. When Al and Gary left the college at the end of the day, Hank called at them, and they all met.

Hank smiled and said to Al and Gary that he had something to tell them. They all went to the Al and Gary's room in the halls of residence, and only when they all sat down, Hank told them that he had received a reply from the girl Al and Gary had contacted before.

Al and Gary looked at each other and smiled. Then, they looked at Hank and asked him a lot of question about what the girl had replied. Then, they stood up, patted him on the back and said to him that he had got a date.

But Hank did not smile. He was very nervous and said that it was going to be his first date. Hank had never had a girlfriend and had never even been on a date with a girl. Al and Gary were telling Hank that he was going to enjoy it and that it was going to be fun.

Then, Hank shook his head and said that he was not going. He said that he was too nervous to go because the girl was expecting someone rich, while he was not rich. He was afraid that the girl would shout at him and tell him that he was a liar and an **imposter**.

When Al and Gary heard Hank complaining about not being rich, they gave him some more money so that he would not look so poor and so he could invite the girl for a drink or dinner.

Hank was not happy about that idea, but because he had already agreed and because he got some more money from Al and Gary, he finally promised to go and meet the girl. When Hank came back home, he replied to the girl that they could meet on Saturday in the Vibe Bar in the **city centre**.

The girl replied soon and agreed to meet Hank in the Vibe Bar in the city centre. Hank and the girl agreed to meet at eight o'clock in the evening. Hank put on his most expensive suit, took all the money he had and went to the bar to meet the girl.

Al and Gary were excited about Hank going on a date with the girl and were looking forward to hearing from Hank about what the date was like.

*

It was Saturday and Al and Gary **stayed up** until late at night, but shortly after they went to bed, they heard a drunk man singing outside the halls of residence. The voice of the singing man seemed very familiar to them, when suddenly, Gary quietly shouted 'Hank!'.

Al quickly woke up, and when they both looked out of the window, they could see that the drunk man who was singing outside the halls of residence really was Hank. Hank was sitting on a bench under a street lamp and appeared very happy. Al and Gary quietly walked out of their room and **unnoticeably** left the halls of residence.

They quickly ran to Hank and asked him what the night with the girl had been like. Hank was very drunk but was excited to talk, and he told them everything. He talked about the girl, how beautiful she was and how much she liked him. He talked about all the fun they had together, and then he said that he and the pretty girl had agreed to meet again.

Al and Gary could not believe that. The girl must have known that Hank was not rich, and they were surprised to hear that the girl wanted to meet Hank again. As Hank talked about the night he had spent with the girl, how amazing the girl had been and what great fun he had, Al and Gary soon started to believe that he must have been exaggerating and **making it all up** because he was drunk. In the end, Al and Gary got bored of Hank **constantly** talking about the girl, and they waved their hand and went back to their room to sleep.

The next day, early in the morning, Hank visited Al and Gary in their halls of residence and told them that he was going to meet the pretty girl again that day. They all talked about the night when Hank met the pretty girl, and Hank told them the same things as the previous night when he had been drunk, sitting in front of the halls of residence.

Al and Gary were shocked to hear that Hank really had another date with the girl, and because they could not believe it, Al and Gary agreed to go out with Hank so that they could see her. Hank was pleased and agreed. He was proud to show his new girlfriend to his two friends.

The girl was **stunning**. She was young and beautiful. She wore beautiful clothes, had a beautiful **hairstyle**, and when she said hello to Al and Gary, they were shaking from being so shy and nervous.

The girl talked about the night when she had met Hank. She talked about how much she had enjoyed the night, how much she liked Hank and that she did not mind that he was not rich because she liked him the way he was.

When the girl talked about the night she had spent with Hank, Al and Gary were looking at her with their mouths wide open and without saying anything. Hank was laughing and drinking, while the girl was smiling and kissing him. Al and Gary **excused themselves** and left Hank with his girlfriend alone.

It was shocking. Al and Gary could not believe that the pretty girl was now Hank's girlfriend and that she liked him even though he was not rich. Al was very sad, because the girl could, maybe, be his girlfriend if he had gone on the date with her instead of Hank.

After leaving Hank with his new girlfriend, Al and Gary went to a pub and talked about it. After they drank a few beers, they decided to go back to the halls of residence. They went to bed early because the next day was Monday and they needed to get up early.

Al could not sleep that night. He was lying in bed on his back with his eyes open. He was thinking about the pretty girl and the fact that she was then Hank's girlfriend. And that all happened because Al and Gary had **made** Hank go and meet the girl. The girl wanted an older man, a rich one, and because Al was **neither**, the girl would probably not want to be with him anyway.

But as Al thought about Hank, the girl and the advert, he suddenly got an idea. His idea was to find another advert where a pretty girl was looking for a man, rich or poor, answer the advert, and go and meet the girl himself.

The next day, when Al finished college, he went to buy a newspaper and ran straight to his room to read all the dating adverts. He was excited and thought that if Hank could have a nice girlfriend who he had met via a dating advert, he could find one as well.

Very soon, Al found an advert he liked. The advert was written by a girl, who described herself as pretty and was looking for a man who she could **settle down** with. Al liked the advert, and even though he did not really want to settle down, he decided to reply.

Al also decided to write the letter by hand to show that he was a **gentleman**. He found a white sheet of paper, took a **brown-ink** pen and slowly wrote the letter as a reply to the dating advert.

When he finished the letter, he put it in an envelope. At that moment, Gary came to the room and asked Al what he was doing. Al explained to Gary that he had found a dating advert where a pretty girl was looking for a man to settle down with, and he decided to reply to it. Gary smiled and asked Al to read the letter to him.

Gary liked the letter and also liked the fact that Al wrote it by hand. When Al put the letter in an envelope again and was ready to write his address on it, Gary stopped him and asked him what address he was going to write there.

Al stopped and thought. Then, he looked at Gary and realised that he could not write the address of the halls of residence because he did not want the girl to know that he was still a student. The reason was that the girl wrote in the advert that she was looking for someone to settle down with. Al would tell the girl that he was still a student and that he lived in halls of residence, but he did not want her to know before their first date. Al was afraid that the girl would refuse to go on a date with him if she knew that he was still a student.

Al was sad and thought about what to do. But then, Gary had an idea: Al could use the address of his parents' home, and at the weekend, if the girl replied, he could go home to visit his parents and collect the letter.

Al smiled and said to Gary that it was a great idea. He wrote his name on the envelope and his parents' address. He closed the envelope, left the room and ran to a post office to post the letter as soon as possible.

Al was excited about the advert and was calling home every day to ask if he had received any letter. Every time Al called home, he only spoke to his mother because apparently his father suddenly had to work overtime and was coming home very late in the evenings.

On Friday, when Al finished school, he ran to the halls of residence where there was a phone and called his mum. When Al's mum answered the phone and Al asked if she had received any letter for him, she replied that she had not received any letter for him.

Al was sad and thought that the girl had decided not to contact him and go on a date with someone else instead – someone who had either replied to her earlier or someone who she believed would be better than him. But Al hoped that he would receive a letter one day soon, and he tried to be patient and call his mum regularly to ask if she had received the letter.

Days passed, and Al was calling home regularly every day after he finished school. But, every day, his mother kept telling him that she had not received any letter for him. The whole week passed, and when Al called his mother on Friday and found out that his mum had not received any letter for him, he believed that the girl had decided not to contact him because she had not been interested in meeting him.

Al thought about the girl and the advert he had replied to for a few more days, but because the girl was not replying back to him, he was slowly forgetting about it until he eventually stopped thinking and worrying about it **altogether**.

One day, not too long after Al had replied to the dating advert, he received a letter. He was surprised to see that he had received a letter at the halls of residence. He looked at the envelope and saw that it was from his mother.

Al suddenly remembered the dating advert and believed that his mum had received a letter for him from the girl from the dating advert and decided to send it to him. Al was very excited and opened the envelope very quickly. Then, he unfolded the letter and started reading.

As soon as Al started reading the letter, he realised that it was not a letter from a girl replying to his letter. The letter was from his mother. As he kept reading, he stopped smiling. In the end, he was shaking.

Gary was lying in bed and watched Al. When he saw how stressed Al was, he asked him what the letter was about. Al dropped the letter, looked at Gary and said that his father had **filed for divorce**. Gary sat up quickly, shocked, and asked Al what the reason was. Al just shrugged his shoulders and answered that his father had found a new woman who he wanted to live with. Therefore, his father wanted to divorce Al's mother.

Al decided to go home at the weekend and speak to his mother. When he arrived home and walked in the house, he met his mum who was sitting on a chair in the kitchen, crying. Al sat next to her and asked what had happened and why his father wanted to divorce her.

His mum shook her head and instead of explaining it to Al, she showed him a letter. The letter was from a girl who wanted to meet Al's father. She wrote in the letter that she was looking for a man who she could settle down with and would like to meet him.

Al suddenly realised that the letter was from a girl who had replied to his letter which he had written to her as a reply to her dating advert. Al's father thought that the letter was for him, replied to it and met the girl. Then, they fell in love with each other, and now, he wanted to divorce his mum.

Al's father's name was also Alfred, but because everyone called Al as Al, not Alfred, he had not realised that when he wrote his name on the envelope as Alfred and then he wrote his parents' address underneath it when he was replying to the dating advert, Al's father must have thought that the letter was for him when the girl replied using the same name and address.

Al hugged his mother and said that he was sorry and that everything would be OK. From then on, Al decided never to reply to any dating advert again.

Vocabulary

dating advert – An advert is a note where people look for something or offer something. A dating advert is a note where people look for a partner.

go wrong – to not succeed; not to be successful

halls of residence – a dormitory; a place where students live during their studies. Halls of residences are provided by universities

single – without a partner

go out (with someone) – to go on a date; to meet someone as a potential partner

shy – not confident

girlfriend – a girl or woman who is in a relationship with a man

date – a meeting arranged in advance, usually with someone you are or might end up in a relationship

textbook – a book written for students to study from

put down – to put away / aside

sit up – You sit up from the position of lying.
– When you sit up in bed, it means that you are lying and then you sit up (you are not lying anymore).

disappointment – dissatisfaction; discontent

demanding – expecting too much; requiring more than usual

catch someone's eyes – to attract attention (because good looking)

out loud – using a voice; not silently

post – to send a letter or parcel using the post office

shake hands – People shake their hands when they clasp each other's right hands to express agreement (or mutual respect).

experiment – the testing an idea

go on a date – to go and meet someone as a (potential) partner or to establish a relationship

in - inside

keep (doing something) – to continue (doing something)

imposter – a person who pretends to be someone else

city centre – the centre of a city

stay up – to stay awake
- When you stay up, it means that you do not go to sleep.

unnoticeably – without anyone's perception / notice

make it all up – to compensate; to repay

constantly – without interruption; non-stop

stunning – very beautiful

hairstyle – the style of someone's hair

excuse oneself – to leave in a polite manner (to say goodbye and leave)

make – to prompt; to persuade; to inspire

neither – not any of both (not older, not rich)

settle down – to become established somewhere (in a place, city, house)

gentleman – a man of good manners (polite) and style (wears good clothes)

brown-ink – When you write with a brown-ink pen, the writing is brown (because the ink inside the pen is of the colour brown)

altogether (in this case) – completely; at all

file for divorce – to ask the court to end someone's marriage

The Return of Bertha's Husband

Bertha was an **elderly** woman who lived with her husband Frank in a small, **solitary** house in the **countryside**. Although Bertha and Frank's house was small, their garden was large. Bertha liked her garden and spent a lot of time there, especially in summer. She had a lot of fruit trees in the garden, and she was growing vegetable and flowers.

At the end of Bertha and Frank's garden, there was a narrow **stream** with a large **meadow** behind it. Frank liked to sit by the stream and watch the water flow. Sometimes, Frank was **fishing** in the stream or had a walk alongside the stream. Not far from their house, there was a small bridge across the stream and when Frank went for a walk, he crossed the bridge and walked in the meadow.

Bertha and Frank lived alone. They never had any children, and because they lived in a **solitary** house in the countryside, they did not have friends. For that reason, they never had any visitors in their house. The only people Bertha and Frank ever talked with were a postman and those they met in a shop in the **nearby** village.

Because Bertha and Frank lived alone, they spent their evenings reading and talking to each other. Recently, though, Frank was very quiet, did not want to speak to Bertha, and did not even want to read. When Frank spoke to Bertha, he was forgetting some words. Also, Frank was sometimes forgetting names of people, what day it was or what he was supposed to buy. Sometimes, Frank got lost when he walked alongside the stream or when he went shopping to the village.

Bertha did not **pay attention** to it and thought that Frank was just getting too old and tired to concentrate. Frank was spending more and more time sitting by the stream, fishing or watching the birds and **dragonflies** flying around. But Bertha did not mind. She loved her garden and was always working there. She liked it when Frank was there with her.

What worried Bertha, though, was that Frank got sometimes lost when he went for a walk alongside the stream. Sometimes, when he got lost, he returned back home the next day in the morning. Once, Frank was missing for two days. Bertha believed that Frank sometimes walked for too long and went too far, and when it got dark, he could not find the way back home.

One day, Frank was sitting by the stream, fishing, and Bertha was **planting** some vegetable in the garden. When Bertha got up to make some tea, she called at Frank in order to ask him if he wanted some tea as well. Frank did not answer. Bertha turned around to call at Frank again, but as soon as she looked towards the stream where Frank had sat, he was not there.

Bertha knew that Frank had gone for a walk again and **swore**. Bertha swore that Frank had gone for a walk because the last time he had gone for a walk alongside the stream, he got lost and returned two days later. He was confused, did not know where he was and how he got there. Bertha made Frank **swear** that he would not go for a walk alongside the stream on his own again.

Bertha hoped that Frank would return soon. She swore again and went to the house to make some tea. From time to time she looked out of the window to check if Frank had come back. In the evening, while Frank was still missing, Bertha went to the stream and called Frank. Because Frank did not answer, Bertha decided to walk along the stream to find him. She was worried that something bad had happened to him, and as she was walking alongside the stream, she was calling Frank's name. Bertha did not find Frank, so in the end, she came back home.

Although Bertha was angry at Frank during the day, she was worried about him during the night. Bertha was worried about Frank at night because he still had not come back. Bertha did not sleep the whole night, and from time to time, she was going outside to the garden with a **torch** to check if Frank had returned. Every time she went out to the garden, she called his name.

In the morning, immediately after **daybreak**, Bertha put on warm clothes and went outside to look for Frank. She walked for **hours and hours**, called Frank's name, but she did not find him. She walked for miles, and when she was exhausted, she returned back home.

At home, Bertha made some tea and sat at the dinner table in the kitchen from where she could see the garden and the stream. Then, she cried and **prayed** for Frank to come back home. Bertha took a **sip** of tea and thought about the previous time when Frank got lost when he had gone for a walk. That time, she was also very worried, but in the end, Frank returned back home. Bertha hoped that this time, Frank would also return and that he would return soon.

Days passed, but Frank was still missing. Bertha was walking alongside the stream looking for Frank every day, but she never found him. In the end, Bertha decided to go to the police and **report** that her husband had **gone missing**. After that, Bertha was walking alongside the stream to look for Frank only from time to time. She knew that the police were looking for him, and she believed that they would find him soon.

*

Nearly two months later, when Bertha still believed that her husband would come back home, someone **knocked on the door** of her house. Bertha believed that it must have been her husband and quickly ran to open the door. Even before she opened the door, she laughed and called Frank's name.

But it was not Frank; it was the police. When Bertha opened the door, the police officer **took off** his hat and told Bertha that they had found a man's body in the stream, not far away from Bertha's house. Then, the police officer said to Bertha that it might have been her husband, and he asked her to go with him to the police station to **identify** the body.

Bertha was convinced that it must have been her husband. She started crying, and the police officer tried to calm her down. When Bertha calmed down a little, the police officer took her to the police station where they kept the dead body of the person they had found in the stream.

Bertha was so convinced that the dead man was her husband, that even before the police officer **uncovered** the body, Bertha called the dead man Frank's name. When the police officer uncovered the body and asked Bertha if she could identify the person, Bertha nodded and said that it was her husband.

When Bertha looked at the dead body at the police station, the police officer noticed that Bertha did not look at it **properly**, and he asked her to look again to make sure that the body really was her husband.

The man Bertha was asked to identify had been dead for a few days, and his face was not clear enough to recognise easily. But Bertha believed that the dead body must have been her husband and did not want to look at her dead husband again and more **closely**. Bertha just nodded to **indicate** that it was her husband and said that she had lived with him all her life and could recognise him without looking at him twice.

The police officer shrugged his shoulders, nodded and wrapped the body in a **shroud**. He was happy that the body had been identified and that he did not have to **investigate** who the dead man was. Then, he told Bertha that the body would be **examined** in order to find out how exactly her husband died. After that, Bertha could **bury** him.

After the examination, the police officer drove Bertha home. Bertha was crying the whole time she was in the car with the police officer, and the police officer did not talk to her. When they arrived in Bertha's house and the police officer stopped the car, Bertha turned towards him and asked him if she could bury her husband in her garden. The police officer put his hand on her shoulder and quietly said that she could. Bertha thanked the police officer, got out of the car and went home.

As soon as Bertha came home, she locked the door, went to the kitchen and looked out of the window. She was looking at the garden and thought where she would bury her husband. After some time, she decided to bury him near the stream where Frank had liked to sit and fish. It was Frank's favourite **spot** in the garden, and Bertha believed that he would like to be buried there.

There was a small wooden **shed** in the garden where Bertha had all her tools for **gardening**. Bertha went to the shed, took a **shovel** and started **digging** a hole, large enough for her husband's body to fit in. Because the ground was near the stream, it was wet and soft and easy to dig. It did not take long and Bertha dug a deep hole where her husband's body would fit.

A few days later, someone rang the bell, and Bertha went to **answer** the door. It was a police officer – the same police officer as the one who had come to see Bertha when they found her husband's dead body. Bertha said hello to him and invited him **in** for a cup of tea.

The police officer accepted, and he followed Bertha to the kitchen. There, Bertha made a cup of tea for both the police officer and herself. The police officer said to Bertha that the examination of her husband's dead body had finished. The cause of death, the police officer said, was that the person drowned. Because the police did not find any **traces** of **violence**, they believed that he was not **murdered**. Therefore, the investigation of Frank's death had finished and the whole **case** had been closed.

The police officer finished the tea and said to Bertha that if she still wanted, the body of her husband could be delivered to her so that she could bury him herself. Bertha agreed and said that she would like to bury her husband in her garden. The police officer did not **object** to that and said that he would arrange the body of her dead husband to be delivered to her house. Bertha thanked the police officer, and the police officer offered her his **condolences**.

It did not take long and the dead man's body was delivered to Bertha's house. The body was not in a **coffin** because Bertha could not afford **one**. Bertha received the body in a shroud. She placed the body with the shroud inside the hole she had dug for her dead husband next to the stream where he used to like to sit. Then, Bertha filled up the hole with all the ground she had **piled up** aside when she was digging the hole.

It was all done and Bertha was happy that her husband was back at home. He was dead, but at least, he was at home. Because Frank was buried in the garden outside the house, Bertha felt as if Frank was always with her and close to her.

Bertha had a small table with two chairs and a bench in the garden. She moved them next to the place where she had buried her husband's dead body, and every time she was sitting there in summer, she felt closer to her husband. She was happy about the decision to bury her husband by the stream because it was a very peaceful place, with a lot of flowers growing around, and she liked to spend a lot of time there.

Soon after Bertha buried her husband, grass started to grow over the place where Frank was buried. After some time, the grass covered the place where Frank was buried completely, and the place looked same as before.

Very soon after Bertha buried the body, she **came to terms** with the fact that her husband was dead, and she was not sad any more. Her life became a **routine**, and although she lived alone, she did not feel lonely. Bertha did not feel lonely because her husband was always close **nearby**.

*

A year passed since Bertha had buried her husband, and her life had gone back to normal. One day, when Bertha was in the garden, someone knocked on the door. Bertha wondered who it might have been and went to answer the door. When she opened the door, there was an old man standing in front of her. The man wore old, dirty clothes, broken shoes, had long, dirty hair and looked like someone who was **homeless**.

When Bertha saw the man, she made a step back and **pushed the door to** a little. She looked at the man closely and asked him what he wanted. The man answered that he was Frank, her husband. To Bertha, the man did not look like her husband and wanted to close the door. But the man stopped Bertha and asked her to hear his explanation as to why he had been gone for so long.

Because the stranger was holding the door and Bertha could not close it, she unwillingly decided to listen to him what he had to say. The stranger was explaining that one day, after sitting by the stream in his garden, he went for a walk alongside the stream but got lost and could not find the way back home. He **walked and walked**, but it was getting dark. As it was dark and he kept walking, he did not know where he was going. And, the more he walked, the farther from his house he was getting.

Then, the stranger went on explaining that one day he found an **abandoned barn** and lived there for several months. Then, one day, he decided to find his home again and started walking through the countryside. After a few weeks of walking and sleeping under trees, he came to a stream and decided to walk alongside it. In the end, he found his house.

Bertha was shocked to hear that. She knew that her husband was dead, buried in her garden, and she did not like it that someone was pretending to be her husband. After a few moments, while the man kept talking about how he had got lost and how he had found his way back home, Bertha was convinced that she did not know the man and that he definitely was not her husband.

Bertha wanted to finish the conversation. She said to the man that it must have been a mistake, that her husband was dead, that she did not know him and that she was sorry for what had happened to him. She said goodbye to him, but as she was trying to close the door, the man pushed the door, prevented Bertha from closing it and kept talking to her.

The man was **begging** Bertha to listen to him and to believe to him, but Bertha was getting scared of the man. She pushed the door hard, closed it, locked it and left the man outside. Bertha was very upset that someone would come over to her and said to her that he was her husband when her husband was already dead.

Bertha knew that when her husband was still alive, he had problems with his memory. She thought about the days when Frank went for a walk and got lost because of his **memory loss** and was sometimes **wandering** around the countryside for days. What the man was saying reminded her of her husband, but she was convinced that the dead man who she had buried in her garden was her husband.

Bertha looked out of the window in order to see if the man was gone. She could not see the man and felt a little relieved. She went back to the garden and slowly forgot about the man.

The next day, early in the morning, while Bertha was still in bed, someone knocked on the door of her house. Bertha got up, put on a coat and went to answer the door. It was the same man as the previous day who had **claimed** that he was Frank, Bertha's husband.

Bertha got scared to see the man again and quickly shut the door. Then, she shouted at the man through the closed door to go away. The man shouted back at Bertha, saying that he was Frank, her husband. And again, he was explaining to her that he had got lost and that it took him a long time to find his way back home.

But Bertha did not answer. She went to the garden, walked to the place where she had buried her husband, **knelt down** and cried. Then, she got up quickly and ran inside her house. She went to the door and looked through the **peephole**. The man was gone. Bertha looked through the window in the **living room** and in the bedroom. She could not see the man anywhere and was a little relieved.

Bertha was not relieved for long; the man was back the next day. When he knocked on the door of Bertha's house, Bertha did not open the door. She looked through the peephole, and when she saw the man again, she shouted at him to go away. The man shouted back at Bertha to let him in and allow him to talk to her.

That day, the man did not leave, but instead, he sat on the road in front of the house and kept looking at the door of Bertha's house. Bertha was getting scared of the man and thought whether she should call the police. In the end, Bertha decided not to call the police and believed that the man would go away soon and never come back.

Bertha could **tell** that the man suffered from memory loss. She knew it because her husband had also suffered from memory loss. The memory loss was the only thing that the man reminded Bertha of her husband. It was the way he spoke, the way he was forgetting words and the way he was getting lost in the countryside that reminded her of her husband. For that reason, Bertha tried to be **sympathetic** to the man.

At night, Bertha was thinking about the man. The more she thought about him, the more the man was becoming familiar to her. For a second, she even thought if it actually could be her husband. But Bertha quickly **dismissed** the idea and believed that the man reminded her of her husband because of the memory loss and the way he spoke. Eventually, Bertha fell asleep.

The next morning, Bertha got up and went to the kitchen to have breakfast. As she was preparing her breakfast, she looked out of the window. She **froze**. What Bertha saw when she looked out of the window from her kitchen was the strange man who had knocked on her door before and claimed to be her husband. The man was sitting by the stream, on the same spot where Frank used to sit when he was fishing.

The spot where the stranger was sitting was where Frank had been buried. And when Bertha saw the man sitting there, she got very angry at him. She ran out of the house, went to the garden, **grabbed** a shovel and quickly walked to the man. When Bertha got to the man, she raised the shovel above his head and shouted at him to leave.

The man turned around, looked at Bertha and asked her who she was. Bertha was shocked. First, the man was claiming that he was her husband, and then, he did not even know her. Moreover, he **had the cheek** to come to her garden and suddenly say to her that he did not know her. The fact that the man did not know Bertha made her even more convinced that he was not her husband.

Bertha got even more angry at that moment and wanted to **scare** the man **away**. She wanted to show the man that she was not afraid of him and that she could be dangerous if he kept coming back to her house.

In order to scare the man, Bertha wanted to show him that she was about to hit him with the shovel she held. She raised the shovel higher above the man's head, but even before she managed to warn him, the shovel slipped out of her hands. As the shovel slipped out of Bertha's hands, it fell on the man's head.

The man fell on his side and lay on the ground. Bertha screamed and quickly touched and shook the man. The man did not move. Bertha knelt down, shook the man again and called at him. But the man did not respond. The man was dead.

Bertha started to shake. She did not know what to do and cried. She moved the man into the shed that was in the garden and went inside her house to think about what to do with the man.

As Bertha thought about what to do with the man, she suddenly fully comprehended that she had killed the man. If she reported it to the police, or if the police found out about him, she would go to prison. The fact that it was an accident was **irrelevant**; she killed the man. Bertha did not want to go to prison and started thinking about how she could **get rid of** the body.

*

Bertha decided that the best way to get rid of the dead man's body was to bury it. As she planned to bury the dead man, she remembered that when she had been burying her husband, the ground by the stream was soft and easy to dig. She, therefore, decided to bury the man there, next to her husband. It was already getting dark outside, but because Bertha had already made a decision to bury the man, she did not want to wait and wanted to bury the man as soon as possible.

She walked to the garden, took the shovel and started digging a hole. She worked quickly and quietly. The night was very quiet, and the only thing she could hear was the water in the stream.

When the hole was large enough for the dead body to fit in, she went to the shed, pulled the man's dead body out and dragged it to the hole. Then, she threw the man into the hole and filled the hole with all the ground she had dug out.

Bertha never spoke about the man with anyone, and soon she forgot about the accident. She never actually forgot about the accident, of course, but she never thought about it. He was a strange man, and she had never known him. Bertha also believed that the man was homeless and did not have any family.

Not long after the accident, when Bertha's life became a routine again, someone knocked on the door of her house. The knocking **made** Bertha **jump**. She tried to calm down before answering the door and smiled. Then, she went to answer the door.

It was a police officer. Bertha got really scared to see the police officer, but the police officer smiled, apologised that he had scared her and just said that he was looking for a man who got missing. Then, he pulled a picture of the man out of his pocket and showed it to Bertha.

Before Bertha saw the picture, she stopped breathing for a moment and turned **pale** in her face. When Bertha looked at the picture, she did not recognise the man. It was a relief to her because she had thought that it would be the man she had killed. It was a man Bertha had never seen before, and that was what she had said to the police officer.

The police officer thanked Bertha and walked away. Bertha closed the door and noticed that she was shaking. She was still stressed about the accident when she had killed the man who had pretended to be her husband.

After the police officer left, Bertha realised that the man in the picture was wearing the same clothes as her husband when he was found dead in the stream. But Bertha thought that it must have been a coincidence;

most people who lived in the area around in the countryside were wearing similar clothes.

It did not take long and someone knocked on the door of Bertha's house again. And again, it was a police officer; the same police officer who had asked Bertha about the missing man. That day, the police officer told Bertha that the man who was missing had liked to take long walks alongside the stream. The police officer believed that the man might have fallen into the stream and might have drowned.

The police officer said to Bertha that they had searched most of the stream in the local area and did not find anything. But a part of the stream belonged to Bertha's garden, and because it was her **property**, the police needed her permission to go and search it. Bertha was shocked and did not like the idea of the police searching in and around the stream that was in her garden.

When the police officer saw Bertha's face, he said that she had nothing to worry about because they just wanted to make sure the man had not drowned and was not in the stream anywhere in or around Bertha's property. When Bertha did not answer, the police officer told her that if she did not agree, they could get a **search warrant** because they had to search the whole local area.

After the police officer said that to Bertha, she looked even more shocked. When the police officer saw Bertha's face, he laughed and said that it would not be necessary because, surely, Bertha would happily allow them to search the stream in her garden. Bertha tried to smile, and in the end she nodded. The police officer smiled and thanked her.

The police officer said to Bertha that he and his **colleagues** would come the next day. He assured Bertha that they would not spend too much time in her garden and that she should not be afraid because she had nothing to worry about. Bertha tried to smile, but it was obvious that she was stressed and that she was shaking. The police officer understood that Bertha was stressed because her husband had once drowned in the stream, and now they wanted to look in the stream for another man who might have drowned.

When the police came to visit Bertha the next day, Bertha opened the door of her house for them and offered them some tea. The police officers thanked her but refused. They only asked Bertha to show them the way to the garden and to the stream. Bertha showed them the way but did not go with them. Instead, she watched them through the kitchen window.

The police officers went straight to the stream and walked alongside it on a small **path**. They walked **there**

and back a few times but did not see anything that would lead to finding the missing man.

When the police officers were leaving the path and were entering the garden, one of the police officers noticed that there was a spot in the ground next to the stream which looked different than the ground around it. The ground of the spot was a little bit raised above the surrounding ground level, and the grass did not cover it completely.

When Bertha saw that the police officers noticed the spot where she had buried the strange man, she went to the garden and explained to the police officers that the spot they were looking at was where she had buried her husband.

The police officers remembered the incident when Bertha's husband had died, and they knew that Bertha had buried him in the garden. The police officers nodded, but one of them found it strange that the ground was still so soft, was still so raised and that grass had not grown over it yet. It was about a year ago when Bertha buried her husband, but the ground looked like it was dug out recently.

After talking among themselves, the police officers made a decision to dig up the dead body and confirm whether it really was Bertha's husband who was buried there.

Bertha did not argue against that. She could not do anything. She could not stop them, and even if she tried, it would all look **suspicious** and make her look **guilty**. In order to look **innocent**, Bertha offered the police officers her shovel. The police officers thanked her, apologised for the **inconvenience** and started digging. In the meantime, one of the police officers called Frank's **dentist** to **come over** and examine the teeth of the dead body in order to confirm that it really was Bertha's husband.

It did not take long and the police officers dug the hole deep enough to find the dead body. The dentist arrived shortly after and started examining the teeth of the dead body. Bertha knew that as soon as the dentist confirmed that the body was not Frank, the police officers would arrest her and investigate why she had a body of a strange man buried in her garden.

Before the dentist was able to start examining the body, the police officers turned the body of the man on its back and cleaned his face. The dentist put on an **apron**, gloves and a **mask** and started examining the dead man's teeth. After a few minutes, the dentist got up, took off the mask and gloves, turned towards the police officers, nodded and quietly said that the dead body really was Frank, Bertha's husband.

At that moment, Bertha screamed and fainted.

Vocabulary

elderly – old; an old person or people

solitary – being alone, standing in isolation

countryside – a rural region; a land or area outside cities and towns.

stream – a small flow of water (resembling a small river)

meadow – a field where grass freely grows

fish – an act of catching a fish

solitary – being alone, standing in isolation

nearby – close; near; not far away (used as an adjective or adverb)

pay attention – to be attentive

dragonfly – a slim insect with long wings

plant – to put a seed of a plant (a flower, tree, vegetable) into the ground

swear
- One meaning of the word 'swear' is to say bad words

- Another meaning of the word 'swear' is to promise

torch – a small portable lamp

daybreak – the first light of a day

hours and hours – a lot of hours (the conjunction 'and' multiplies the meaning of the words it connects)

pray – to address God (by saying a prayer)

sip – to have a drink a little

report – to give information; a short account of the news; the act of informing

go missing – when someone gets lost, they go missing

knock – to tap or hit loudly enough to be heard when someone wants to attract attention
– You knock on a door when you want someone to open the door.

take off – to remove a piece of clothes

identify – to establish the identity of someone

uncover – to remove a sheet in order to reveal

properly – well enough; with enough attention

closely - well enough; with enough attention

indicate – to show; to express briefly

shroud – a burial piece of cloth for a dead body to be wrap in

investigate – to carry out a systematic inquiry to discover facts

examine – to observe or look over closely

bury – to place in the ground
- When someone dies, they are buried by being placed deep in the ground.

shed – a small wooden shelter as a storage

gardening – the activity or working (cultivating) in a garden

shovel – a tool for digging (making) holes in the ground

dig – to make a hole in the ground (usually with a shovel or spade)

answer – You answer the door when someone rings the bell and you go to open the door to see who it is.

in – inside

trace – a mark, object or other indication

violence – the act of aggression

murder – the act of killing someone

case – a legal action

object – to protest; to disagree

condolences – an expression of sympathy

coffin – a box for a dead body to be put in before buried in the ground

pile up – to gather on one side and stack into a pile / heap

come to terms – to be reconciled; to make it up; to accept something as the truth

routine – something that is happening regularly and repeatedly as a habitual method of procedure or life

nearby – close; near; not far away (used as an adjective or adverb)

homeless – a person who has nowhere to live and is on the street

push the door to – to close the door, but not completely – leave it ajar (open slightly)

walk and walk – to walk a lot (the conjunction 'and' multiplies the meaning of the words it connects)

abandoned – left alone, not owned by anyone

barn – a farm building for storing grain or housing farm animals

beg – to ask humbly, eagerly and earnestly; to plead; to implore

memory loss – the fact of losing the ability of remembering information

wander – to walk slowly away from a fixed point or place

claim – to state / say that something is true

kneel down – to get down bending knees

peephole – a hole in a door for someone inside a building to see through

living room – the main room in a house where people

tell – distinguish; to recognise the difference

sympathetic – to show sympathy (similar feelings)

dismiss – to stop considering

grab – to take or grasp quickly or suddenly

have the cheek – to be impudent; to be insolent

scare away – to make someone scared (frightened) in order for them to move away

irrelevant – having no connection with the subject

get rid of – to dispose of; to do away with

make jump – to get scared

pale – white; with no colour; without blood

property – what someone owns such as a house

search warrant – a lawful authorization for searching / looking through someone's property / house

colleague – A person who works with you is your colleague

path – a small way / route / lane created by people (or vehicles) where they walk, created by walking

there and back – from one place to another

look suspicious – to appear or to make an impression that someone is involved in an illegal activity; to appear guilty

guilty – responsible for wrongdoing or an illegal activity

innocent – not guilty of crime
- If you are innocent, you have not done anything wrong.

inconvenience – a difficulty that causes anxiety; the state of being difficult with someone's comfort

dentist – a person who treats / looks after someone's teeth

come over – to come to a place (to visit someone) for a short period of time

apron – a piece of clothing that is tied about someone's waist and worn to protect someone's clothing

mask – a protective covering worn over the face

Twin Brothers and a Pretty Woman

It was not a great day for Gus. He worked as a taxi driver, and that day he did not have many customers and did not earn much money. Moreover, Gus also had a **puncture** and had to use the **spare wheel**. Because of that, Gus had to buy a new **tyre** the next day because he was not allowed to drive his taxi car on a spare wheel.

When Gus came home that day, his wife was complaining about him. She was telling him that he was **useless** and that he was a bad driver. She was angry at him and did not cook dinner for him. When she went to bed, she asked Gus to sleep on the sofa because she did not want to sleep next to someone who could not even make **decent** money. Gus **lowered his head**, nodded and watched his wife go to the bedroom while he was going to lie down on a sofa in the living room.

Gus had always been unlucky, and every time he was doing something, things were **going wrong**. That was his life: he did not like his job, he did not earn good money because he did not have enough customers, he was often unlucky, bad things were happening to him, and his wife did not love him and was complaining about him all the time.

Gus had a twin brother whose name was Carl. Carl, same as Gus, was in the late forties but was **single** and lived **on his own**. Although Carl had a girlfriend **from time to time**, he never took any of the relationships seriously, and no relationship with any of his girlfriends lasted more than a few months.

Carl liked living on his own and was very happy with his life. He was happy that he was not married especially after talking to his brother Gus who had always been complaining to him about his wife. Every time Gus was telling his brother about how much his wife was complaining about him, how she was shouting at him, how she did not want to cook for him and how she did not want to sleep in one bed with him, Carl was smiling, nodding and saying to Gus that he did not have such problems because he was single.

Gus and Carl lived near each other, and they were meeting very often, usually at the weekends. One day, when Gus and Carl met, Gus was, as usual, complaining about his wife and how unhappy he was. While Gus complained to Carl about his wife, Carl suddenly got an idea.

Carl **was seeing** a very pretty woman from time to time, and his idea was that he could arrange a meeting with her, and then, he and Gus could swap. What he meant was that Gus could go on a date for at least one day with the girl Carl had been seeing. That, as Carls said to his brother, would help Gus to relax and **take his mind off things**. Also, being with another woman would help Gus **rethink** if living with his wife was **worthwhile**.

Gus was shocked to hear that. He did not like the idea of cheating on his wife, especially by meeting his brother's girlfriend. But Carl smiled and said that the girl was not his girlfriend, but a woman he had been meeting from time to time, and it would not be cheating because he could just meet her and have a **chat**. Then, he gave Gus a picture of the girl and said to him that if he wanted to meet the girl, all he needed to do was to call him. Before Carl left, he told Gus to think about it overnight and let him know the next day.

Gus looked at the picture of the girl and was shocked to see how pretty she was. At the back of the picture was a name of the girl: Janice. Then, Gus looked at his brother and did not know what to say. Carl smiled at his brother, patted him on the back and said goodbye to him. when Carl left, Gus looked at the picture of the girl again.

The girl in the picture was very pretty. She had long, dark brown hair, light brown eyes, smooth skin and perfect, white teeth. Gus could not stop looking at her, and he kept looking at the picture all the time he walked home. When he came home, he put the picture into his pocket. Then, he took a shower and went to bed. When he closed his eyes, he was imagining the girl and was thinking about her.

The next day, as soon as Gus woke up in the morning, he thought about the girl from the picture. He got up, took the picture of the girl out of his pocket and gave it a long look. As he kept looking at the girl, he decided to visit Carl and speak to him about meeting her.

When Gus was ready to leave and visit his brother, his wife was still in bed. Gus told her that he wanted to go for a walk and visit his brother. Gus's wife quietly **mumbled** something, still half asleep, and Gus left.

As soon as Gus left home, he pulled the picture of the girl out of his pocket, and as he walked, he kept looking at it. He could not believe that his brother had been meeting such a beautiful girl. Gus also thought that spending one day or one night with the girl would really make him happy.

Gus knocked on the door of his brother's house. Carl opened the door, smiled at Gus and invited him **in**. Carl was having breakfast at that moment and shared it with his brother who had not eaten yet. Then, Carl said to Gus that he had already been waiting for him. Gus was surprised to hear that, but Carl said to him that he knew him well enough and knew that he would want to meet the girl. Gus nodded, bent his head and said that he would like to meet up with the girl.

Gus did not feel good about meeting up with his brother's girlfriend, but Carl explained to his brother again that she actually was not his girlfriend. In fact, he had met her only twice, and he did not want to build any relationship with her because he wanted to stay single. And the girl felt the same about the relationship with Carl. Gus did not understand why his brother did not want to be in a relationship with such a beautiful girl but did not ask.

Carl worked as a **retail manager** in a small furniture store. He enjoyed his job and was always the **first one in and the last one out**. In other words, Carl was the first one who opened the shop in the morning and was the last one who closed the shop in the evening.

Carl and Gus agreed to meet in the furniture store the next day in the evening when the shop would be already closed. Carl said to Gus that if they met in the furniture shop, his wife would not find out. If Gus met the girl somewhere in town, Gus's wife could see them. Gus thought about it and eventually agreed to meet the girl in the furniture store where Carl worked.

Gus was nervous to meet the girl, but Carl said to Gus that he knew him because they were brothers and knew that it would be easy for him to pretend to be Carl. Carl then quickly told Gus everything **relevant** about the girl.

Carl told his brother what the girl liked, what she did not like, what she already knew about him and how she liked to be called. Also, Carl said to Gus that Janice did not know that he had a brother. Therefore, Janice would believe that Gus was Carl and would not **suspect** anything.

The next day in the evening, Gus drove to the furniture store where his brother Carl worked and where they had agreed to meet. When he arrived, he parked his taxi car at the car park and walked into the store. When it was time for Carl to close the store, he **left** the keys **with** his brother. Then, Carl patted Gus on his back and left the store.

Janice, the girl Gus was waiting for, arrived in the furniture store a few minutes after Carl had left. When Gus saw Janice enter the store, he stood up and stared at her with his mouth **wide open**. Janice was more beautiful in reality than in the picture.

As soon as Janice entered the store, she said hello to Gus, believing that he was Carl. Gus tried to look confident and acted like his brother in order for Janice to believe that he was Carl.

Gus and Janice started talking, and Gus enjoyed the time with Janice so much that he **lost track of time**. They talked and drank wine until very late at night. In the end, they both fell asleep in a small bed which Carl had in his office. Gus completely forgot that he had not said to his wife that he would not come home that night.

Because Gus was with Janice in the furniture store and did not come home that night, his wife was worried about him and thought that he might have had an accident. For that reason, when it was late at night, she put on a warm **cloak**, grabbed a **torch** and went outside to look for her husband.

Gus's wife walked around the town for hours until she finally **spotted** her husband's taxi car. Gus's wife was surprised to see her husband's car parked outside a furniture store where Gus's brother worked. First, she thought that her husband visited his brother in the shop and for some reason they stayed there until late. Maybe Gus was looking for some new piece of furniture, she though.

But the lights in the shop were off. Gus's wife came closer to the shop and looked inside through the shopping windows. First, she could not see anything, but when she looked inside through the Carl's office window using her torch, she noticed her husband sleeping there in Carl's bed with a woman next to him.

At first, Gus's wife was confused because she was not sure if the man inside was her husband or Carl. But Carl did not live far away from the furniture store so Gus's wife decided to go and see if Carl was at home. When

Gus's wife came to Carl's house, she wanted to knock on the door and speak to him, but because Carl still had the lights on in his house, she decided to look inside his house through the one of the windows. There, she saw Carl, smoking a cigar as usual and watching TV. Gus did not smoke cigars and did not like watching TV so late at night. She knew that it was Carl. That meant that the man in the furniture store must have been Gus.

Gus's wife was not angry. She was shocked and very sad. She suddenly realised that her husband was cheating on her, and she believed that he wanted to leave her. She turned around and walked away from Carl's house.

She walked slowly, and the whole way home she cried and thought about the days when Gus had been coming home very late, saying that he had a lot of customers. She believed that Gus had been cheating on her for a long time.

When Gus's wife came home, she lay in bed and **cried and cried**. She believed that when Gus now had a new girlfriend, he was going to leave her. She was scared. She did not want to be alone and realised that she actually still loved him. Eventually, she **fell asleep**.

When Gus's wife woke up in the morning, she called to the company where she worked and told her **boss** that she did not feel good and could not go to work. Instead of going to work, she spent all morning cooking Gus's favourite food. She believed that Gus would come home, and she wanted to make Gus very happy and wanted him to love her again.

When Gus woke up in the furniture store next to Janice, he felt very happy. But he suddenly **sat up**, looked at his **watch**, **swore** and quickly got up. His brother needed to open the shop soon, and he needed to leave as soon as possible. He woke up Janice and they quickly got dressed. Then, still pretending that he was Carl, he kissed Janice and said to her that he needed to open the shop. Janice smiled at him, nodded and left.

Gus did not go home immediately after Janice left. It was no point of **rushing**. He had spent the whole night out of his house so it did not matter if he came home a little bit later. His wife, Gus believed, did not care about him anyway and was probably happy that he had not been at home the previous night. Instead of going home, Gus waited for his brother in the furniture store.

When Carl came to the furniture store in the morning, Gus was sitting in Carl's chair in his office. Carl closed the door of the office behind him and quickly asked Gus what his night had been like and how he liked Janice.

Gus told his brother everything. He told him about what they talked about, he told him things about her and how much he liked her, and then he said that they fell asleep together in his small bed. Gus said to Carl about how happy he was and how much he had enjoyed the whole time with Janice.

Although Gus liked Janice a lot, he did not want to meet her again. He was still in love with his wife and did not want to be meeting another woman. Carl understood, nodded and said to Gus that he had made a good decision. Then, Gus said goodbye to his brother, thanked him again and left the furniture store.

Gus drove slowly across the town and decided not to work that day. Instead, he wanted to go home and think about the previous night he had spent with Janice. He also wanted to think about his wife. He felt guilty for having spent the previous night with another woman, but he had enjoyed it and did not regret it.

As Gus drove home, he also thought about an excuse he would say to his wife about not having been at home the previous night. Gus had never spent the whole night out of his house and decided to say to his wife that he had been driving, looking for some customers around the local airport.

But Gus did not think too much about excuses. His wife did not care much, and he believed that she would not ask him anyway. Instead, what Gus was thinking about much more was what food he would cook at home because he was very hungry. First, he thought about his favourite meals, but then, he thought about what ingredients he had at home and what he would actually be able to cook.

Gus parked in front of his house, and as soon as he got out of his car, he smelled nice food. He stopped, closed his eyes for a moment, and was imagining the lovely food he smelled. Soon, he realised that it was his favourite meal and was suddenly hungrier than ever before. As Gus was getting closer to his house, the stronger the smell of the food was. It was only when he opened the door of his house that he realised that the nice smell of delicious food was coming from his house.

As Gus opened the door of his house and smelled the food, he stopped. If Gus could smell the food in his house, that meant that his wife must have been at home. Gus was shocked to find out that his wife was at home and did not go to work. He slowly walked to the kitchen where he saw his wife cooking.

As Gus entered the kitchen, he stopped and looked at his wife without saying anything. He did not understand why his wife was at home, why she was cooking and why she was cooking his favourite food. Gus's wife did not know about Gus standing behind her, and Gus took the opportunity to just watch his wife silently. He felt very calm, and for some reason he thought about the old times when they used to laugh together and did not argue.

When Gus's wife turned around and saw Gus standing by the door, she got scared and jumped. She did not expect to see her husband there. But a few seconds later, she ran towards him and hugged him.

Gus's wife acted so fast that Gus did not have time to react and did not know why his wife hugged him. When his wife looked at him, Gus noticed that she was crying. Gus lightly touched his wife's shoulders and asked her what had happened and why she cried.

They both sat down to a dining table in the kitchen and Gus's wife told Gus everything. She told him about having seen him sleep next to another woman in Carl's office in the furniture store where he worked. Then, she told him that she loved him and did not want him to leave her. She promised to be nice to him, to cook for him his favourite meals and never to argue with him.

Gus was shocked to hear that. Normally, he would think that his wife would be angry at him after seeing him with another woman, and he would expect that she would want to leave him. But, instead, she was afraid that he would leave her. Gus's wife was crying and begging Gus to stay with her.

Gus leaned back in the chair, put his hands behind his head to make himself more comfortable and smiled. He was happy again.

Vocabulary

twin – being two identical

puncture – pierced and empty / flat (without air)

spare wheel – an extra wheel in a car ready to be used in case of a puncture on a working wheel

tyre – a rubber covering of a wheel

useless – good for nothing; not useful

decent – (in this case) enough;

lower someone's head – to look down in embarrassment

go wrong – to not succeed; not to be successful

single – not in a relationship; not married

on his own - alone

from time to time - sometimes

be seeing someone – to be meeting someone; to be visiting someone; to be dating someone

take mind off things – to forget temporarily and relax

rethink – to think again

worthwhile – to have a specific value; worth something (the time, money, effort, etc.)

chat – an informal conversation

mumble – to speak indistinctly / unintelligibly

in – inside

retail manager – a person who is in charge or a retail (store)

first one in and the last one out – When you are the first one who comes somewhere (to work for example) and are the last one who leaves the place, you are first one in and the last one out.

relevant – having a connection with the subject

suspect – to think / imagine that something is the case / is true

left something with someone – to give something to someone to keep it for some time

wide open – fully open

lose track of time – to lose the grasp / awareness of what the time is

cloak – a loose outer piece of clothing

torch – a small portable lamp

spot – to notice; to see

cry and cry – to cry a lot (the conjunction 'and' multiplies the meaning of the words it connects)

fall asleep – to start sleeping

boss – a person who is in charge of workers

sit up – You sit up from the position of lying.
– When you sit up in bed, it means that you are lying and then you sit up (you are not lying anymore).

Watch – a small clock worn on a wrist

swear – to say bad words

rush – to do something or to move quickly

CPSIA information can be obtained
at www.ICGtesting.com
Printed in the USA
BVHW051918140622
639782BV00012B/148